Footy shorts
THE LITTLE COLOURING BOOK

Printed in the United States of America

Bogan blokes in footy shorts deserve some attention.

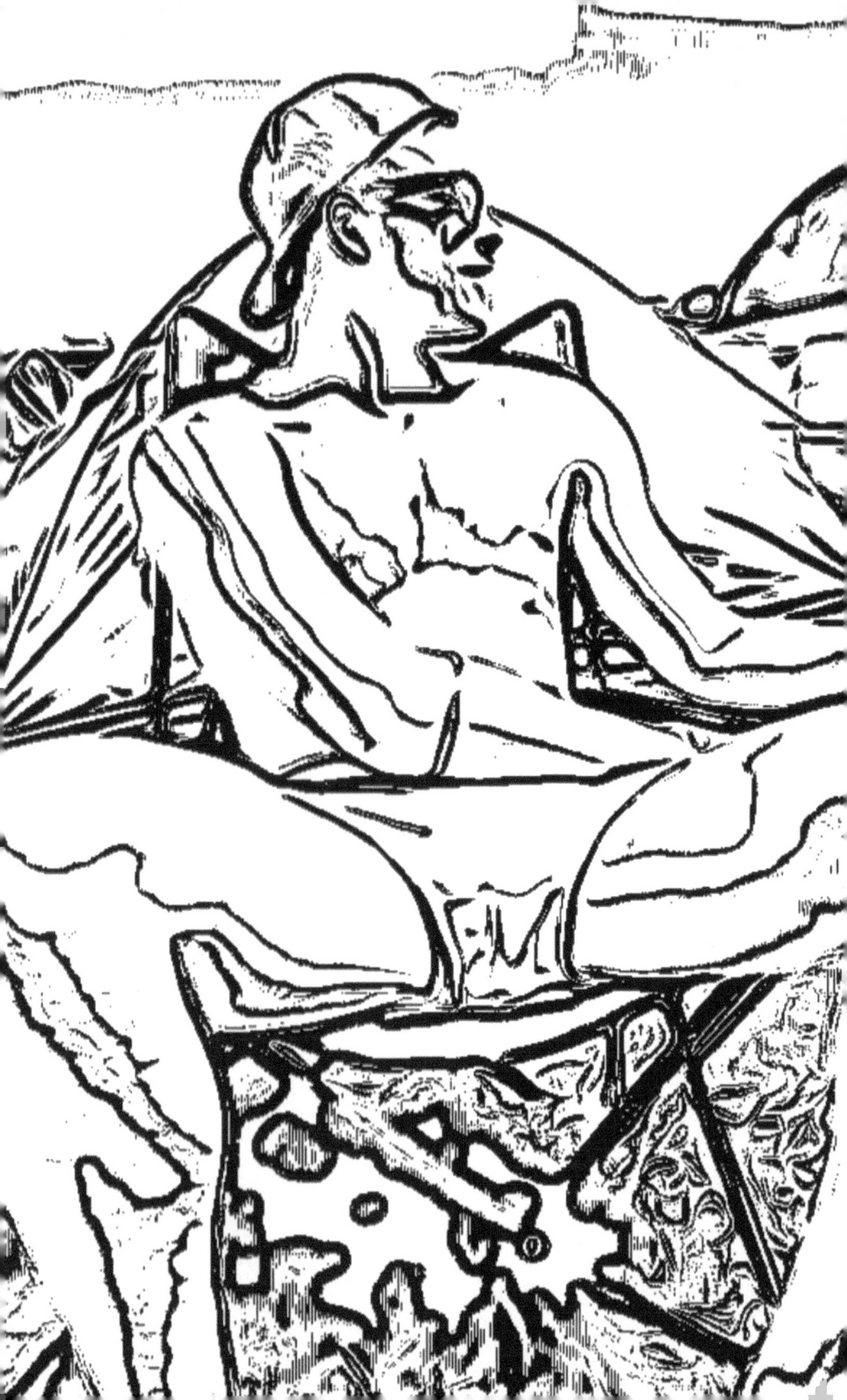

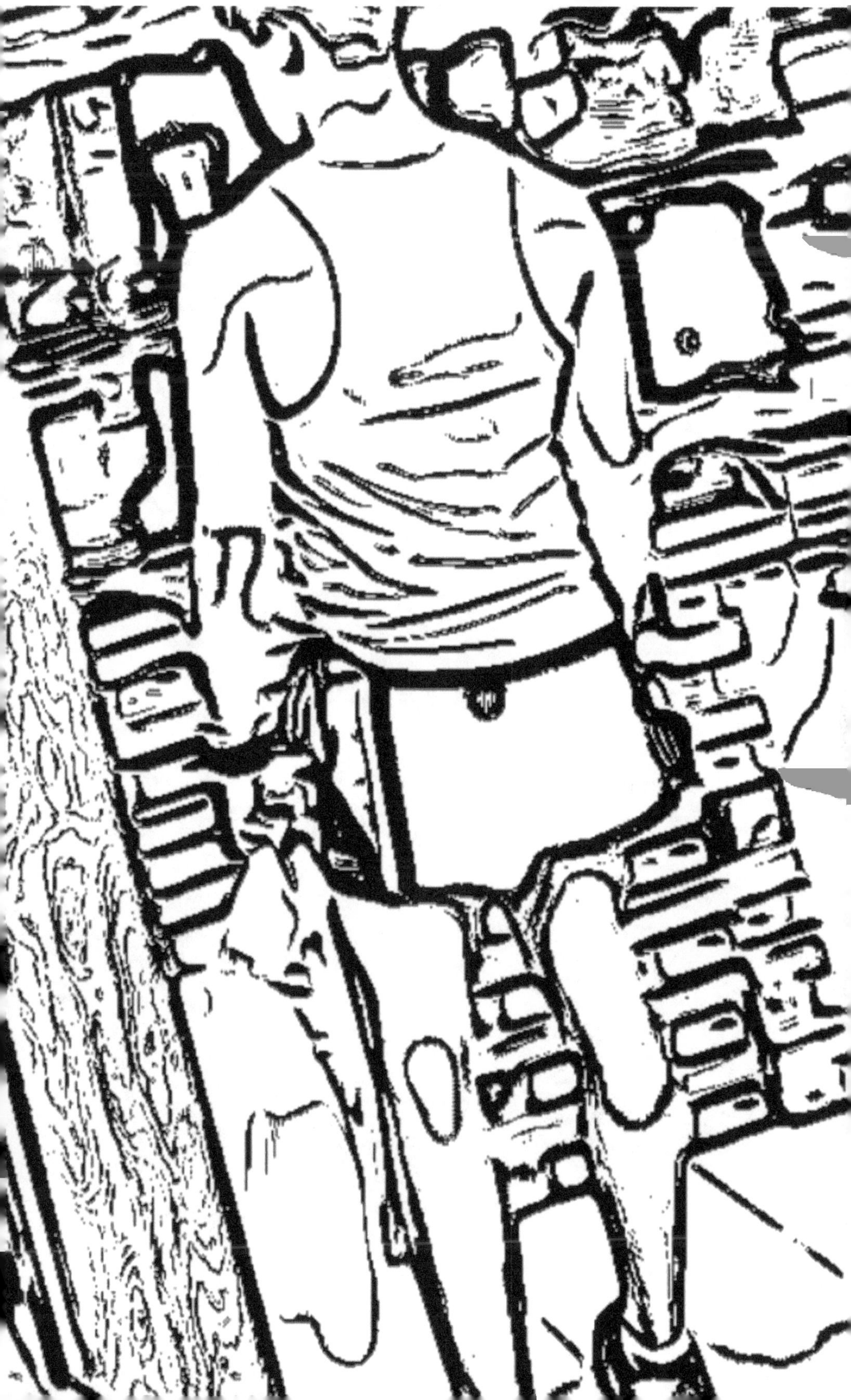

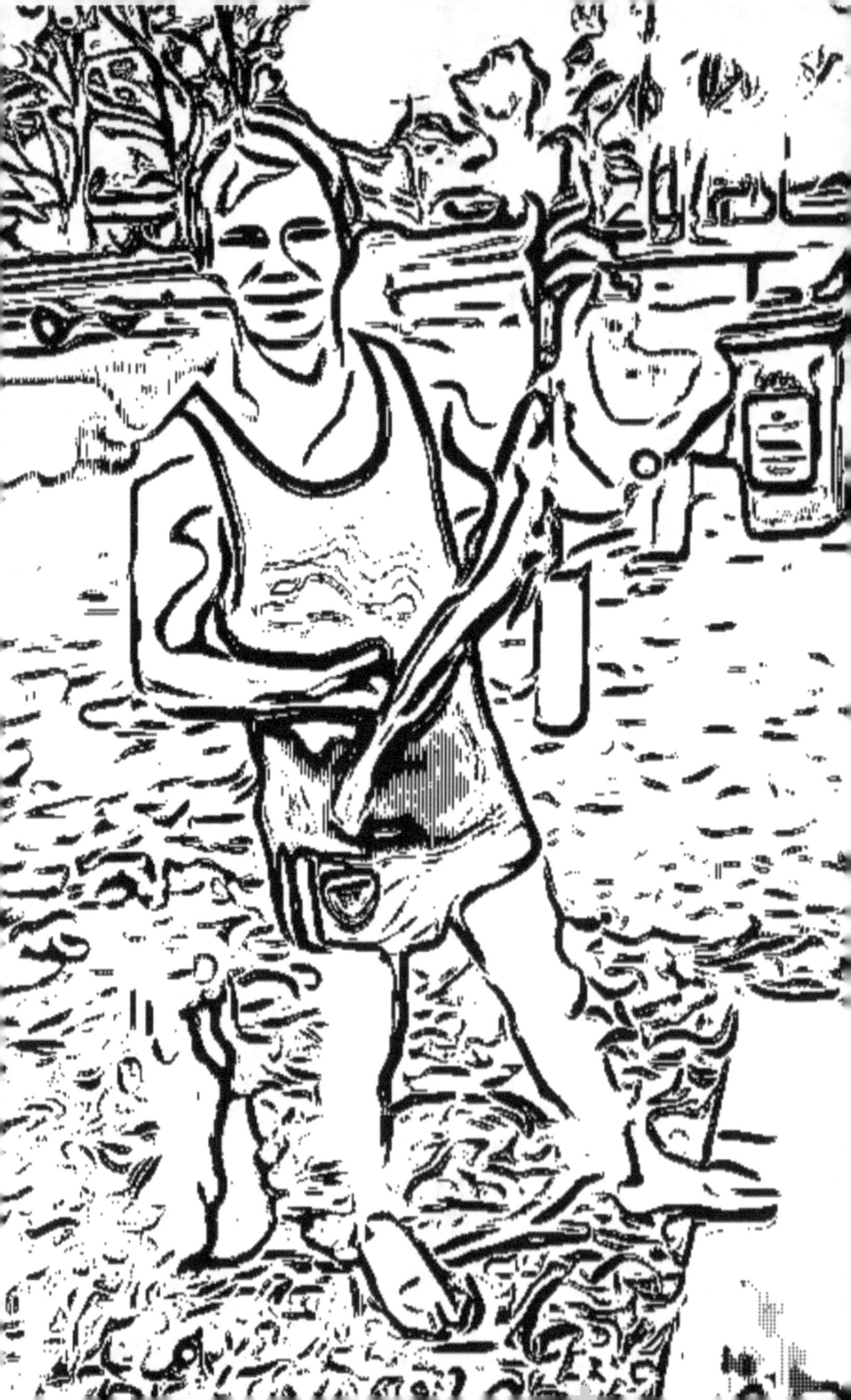

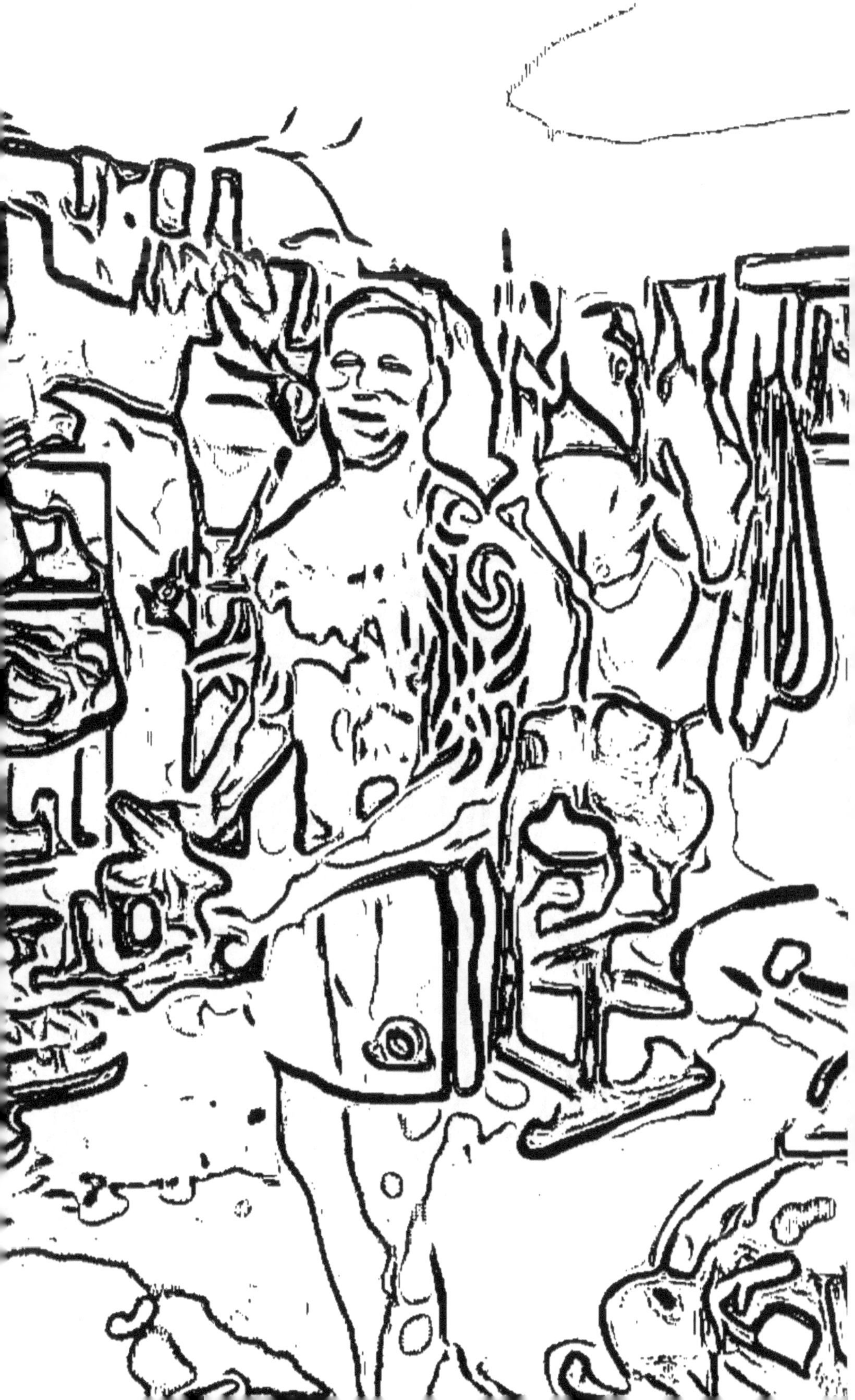

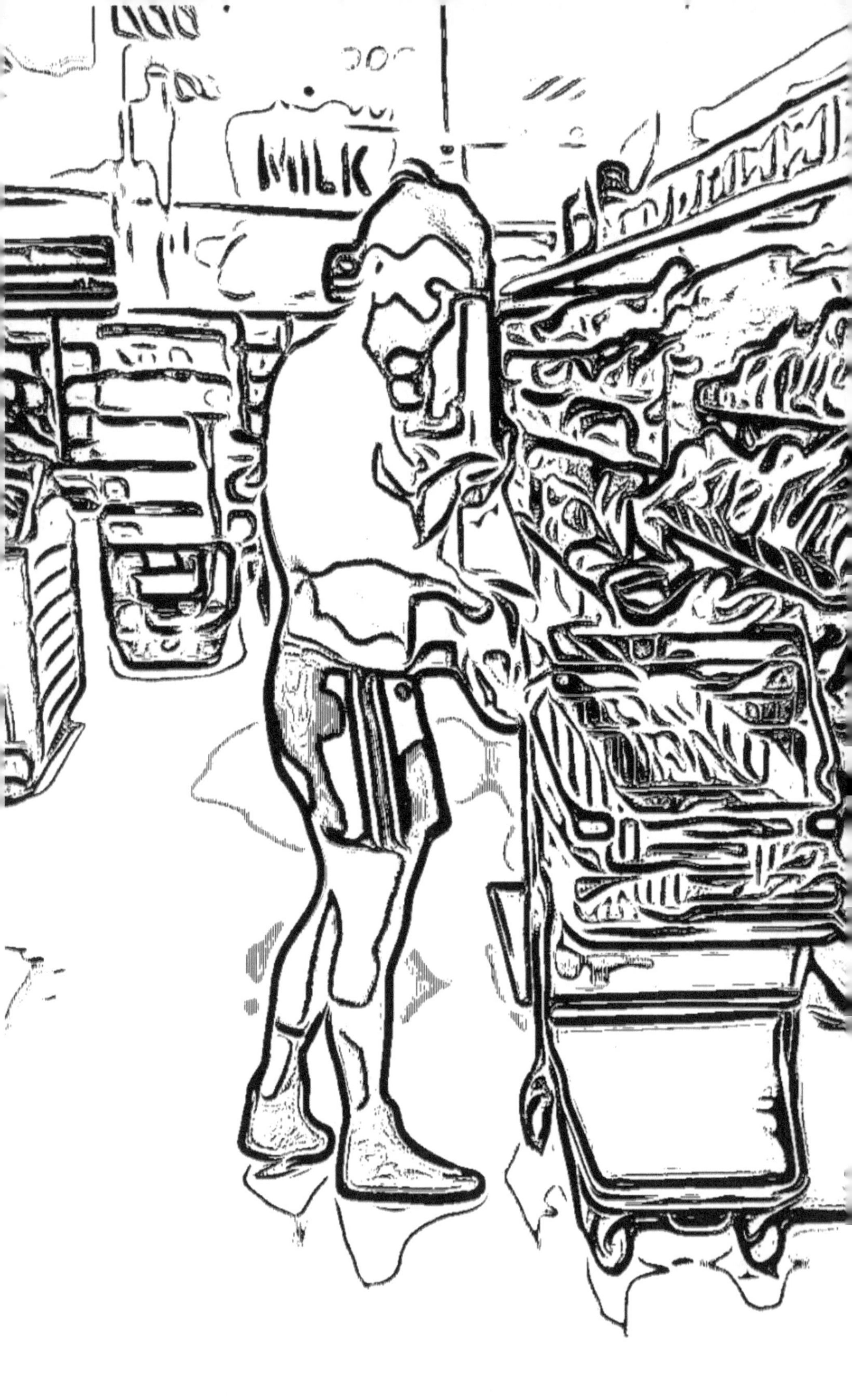
MILK

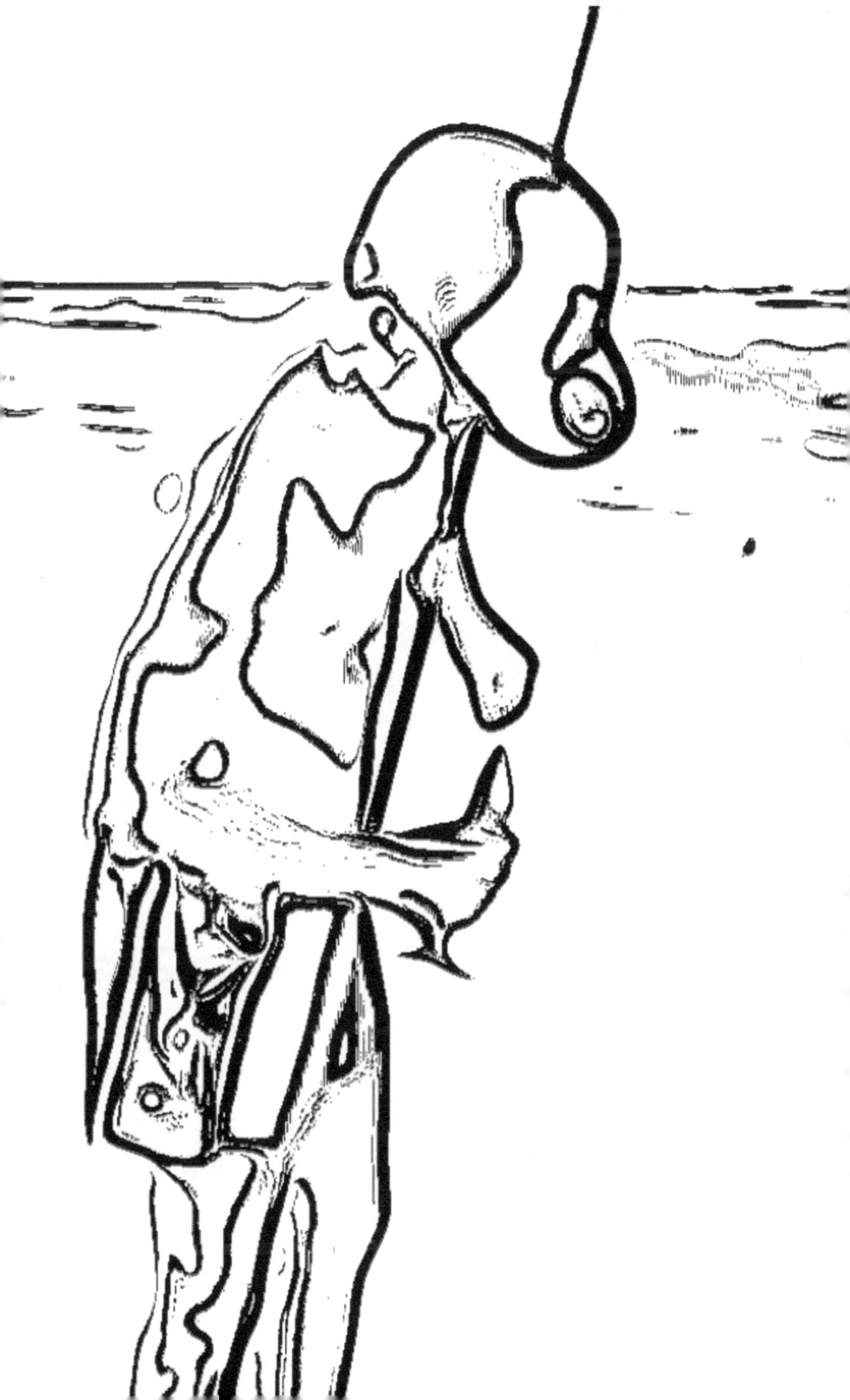

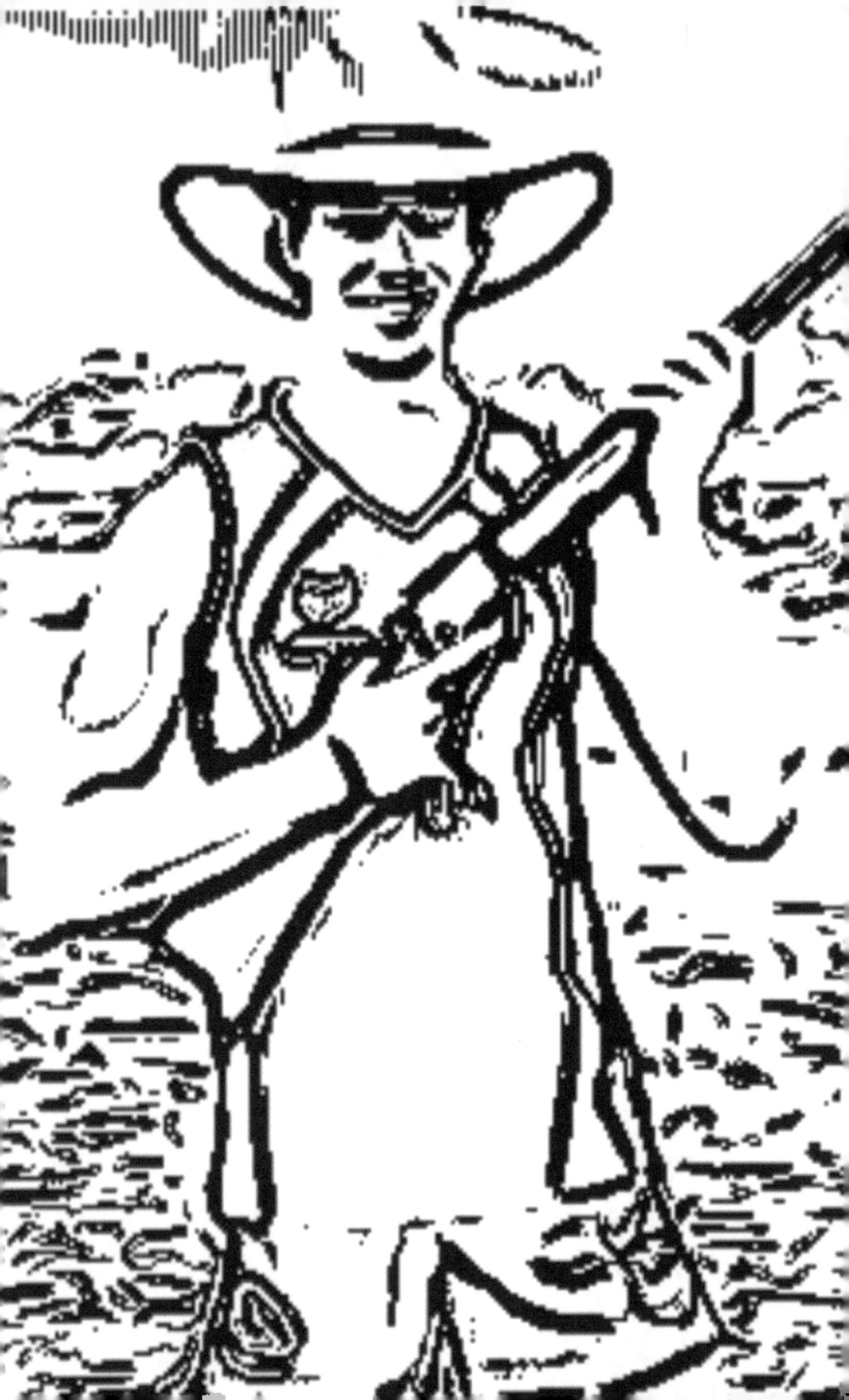

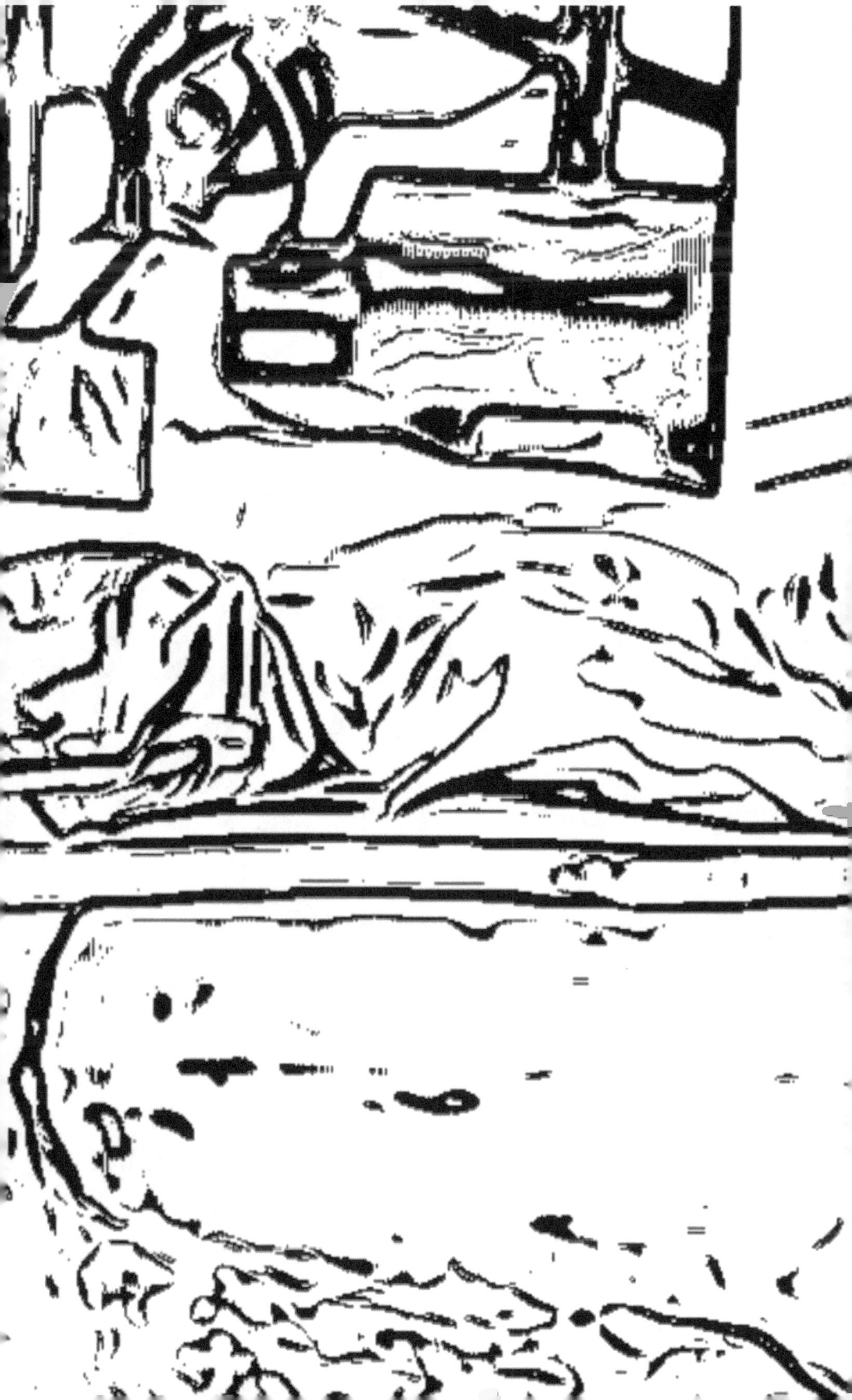

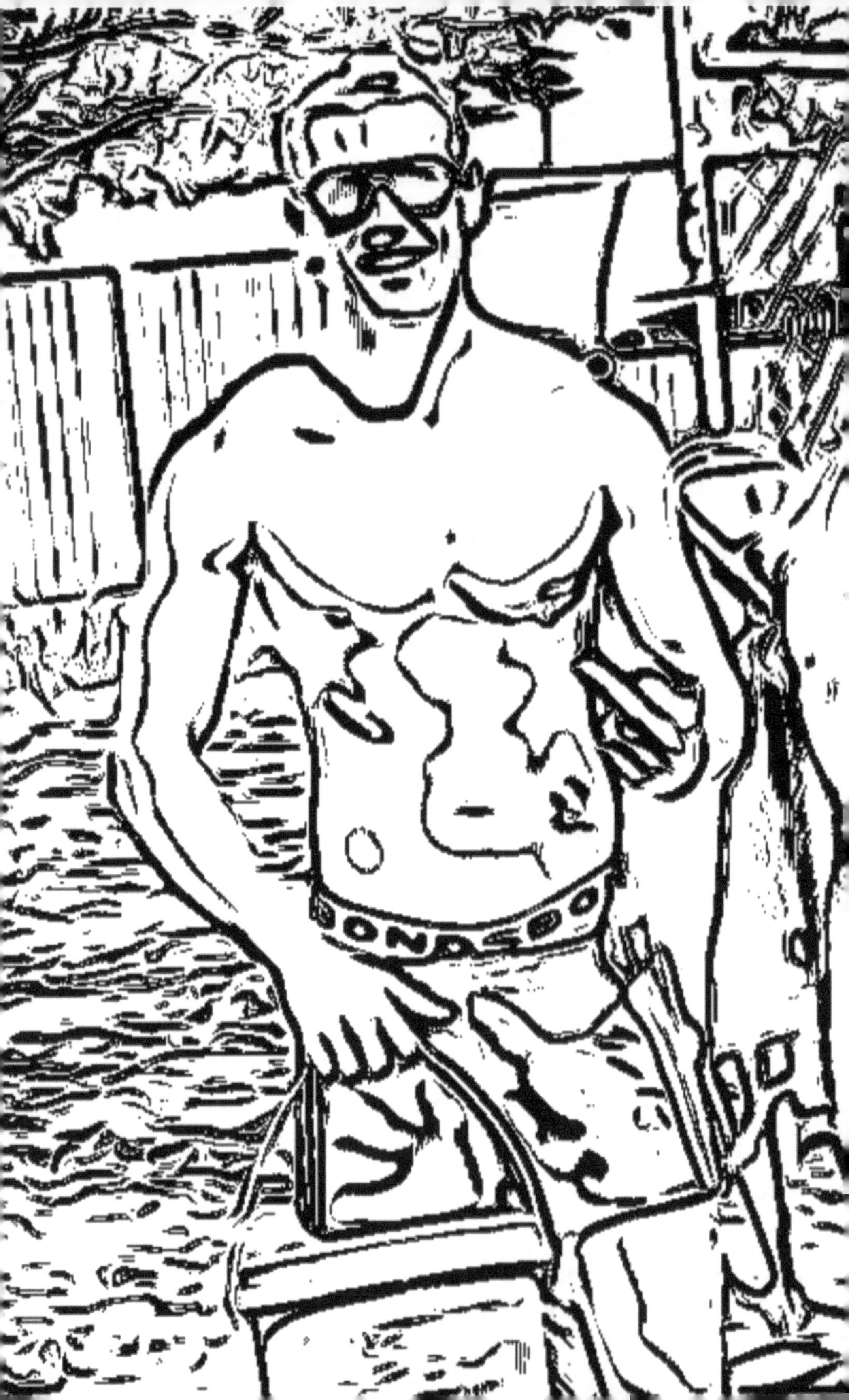
BONDS BO

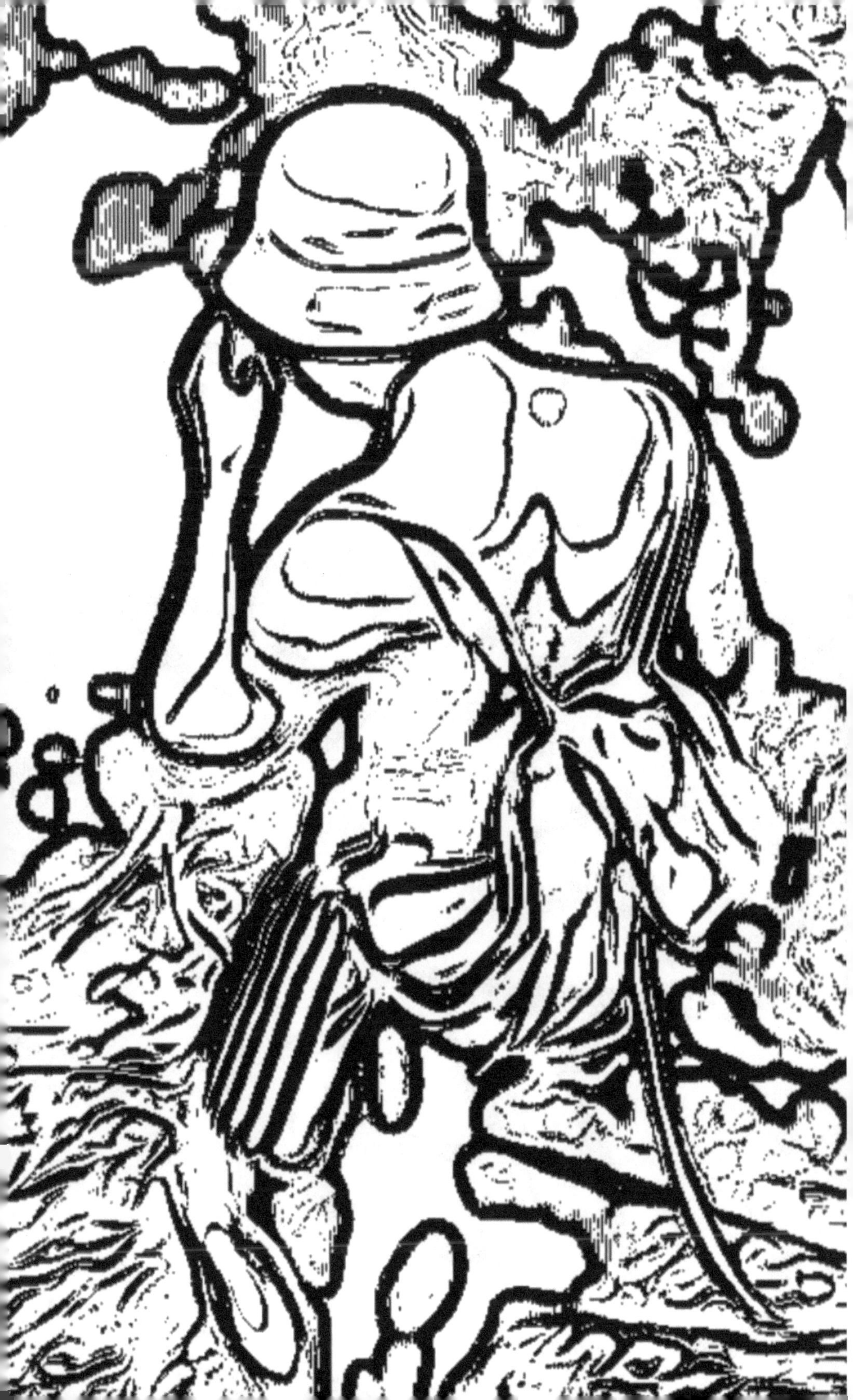

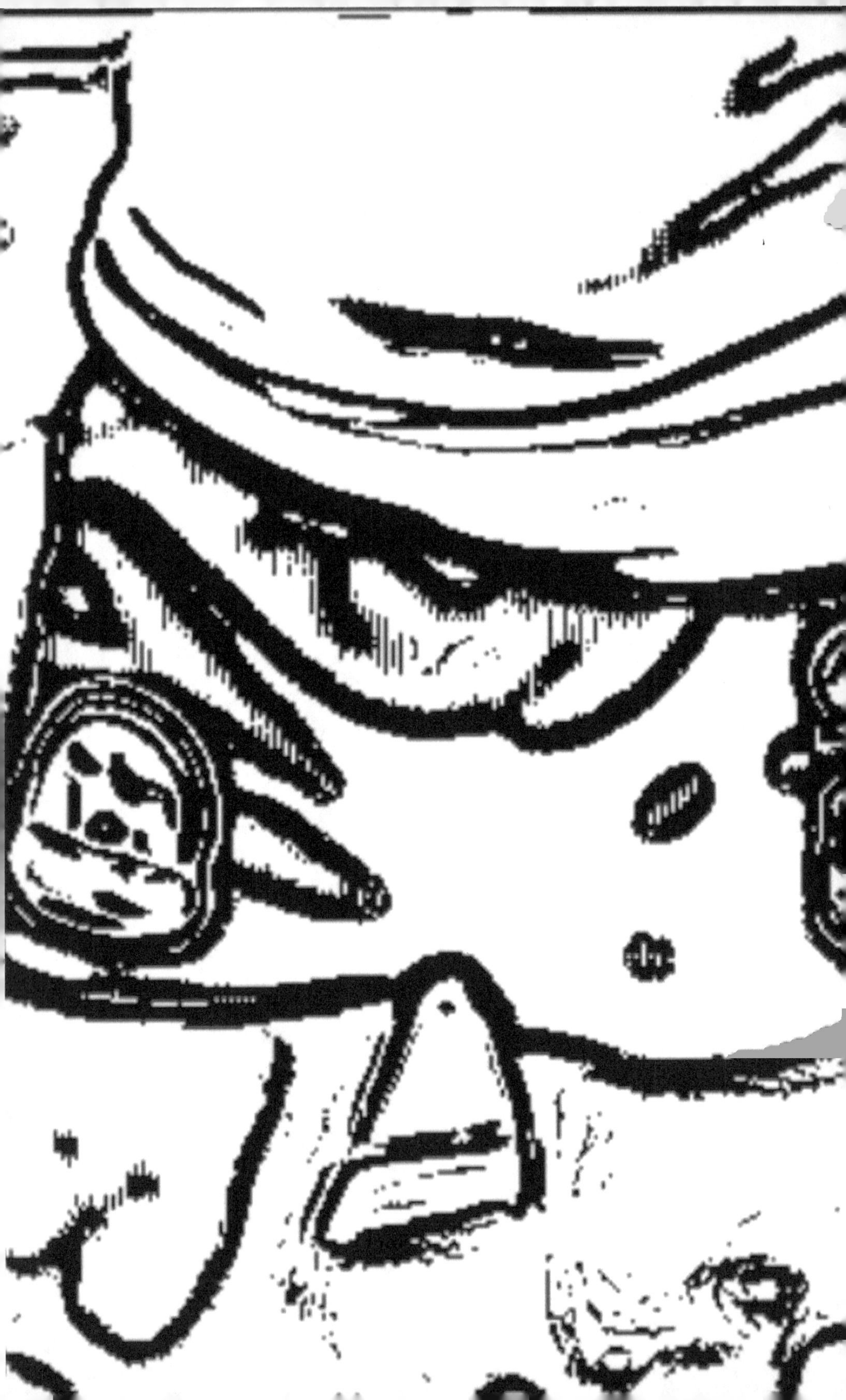

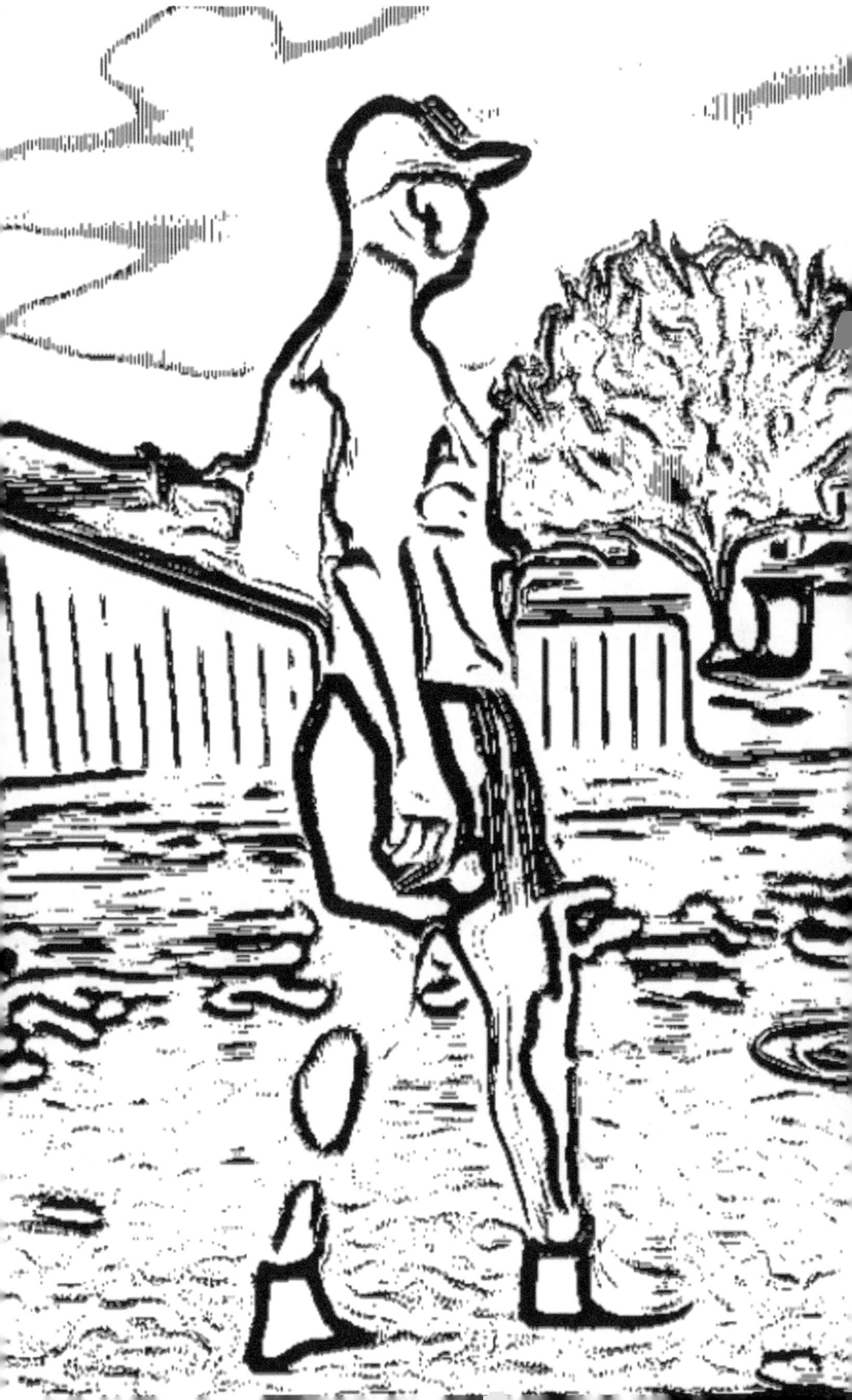

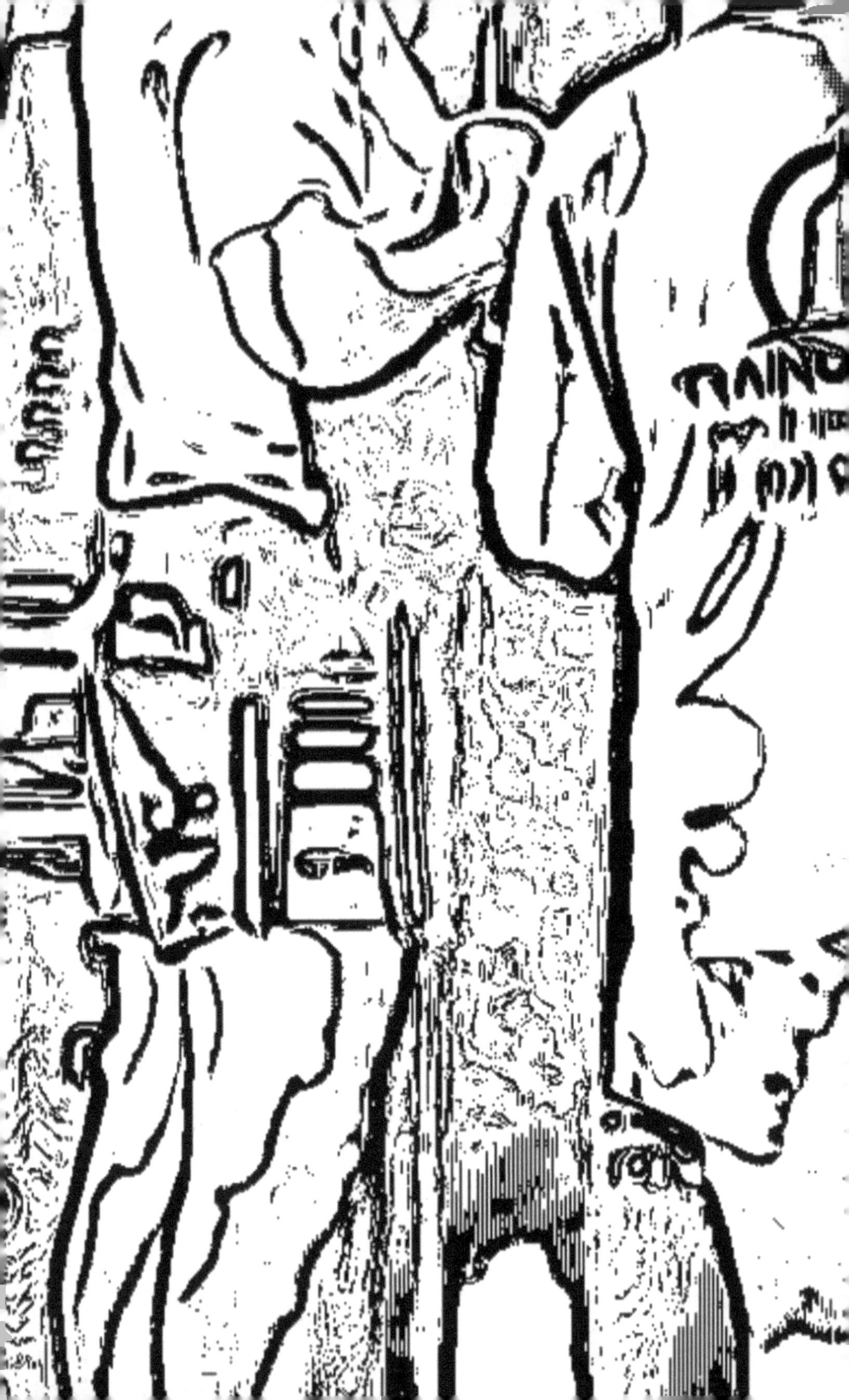

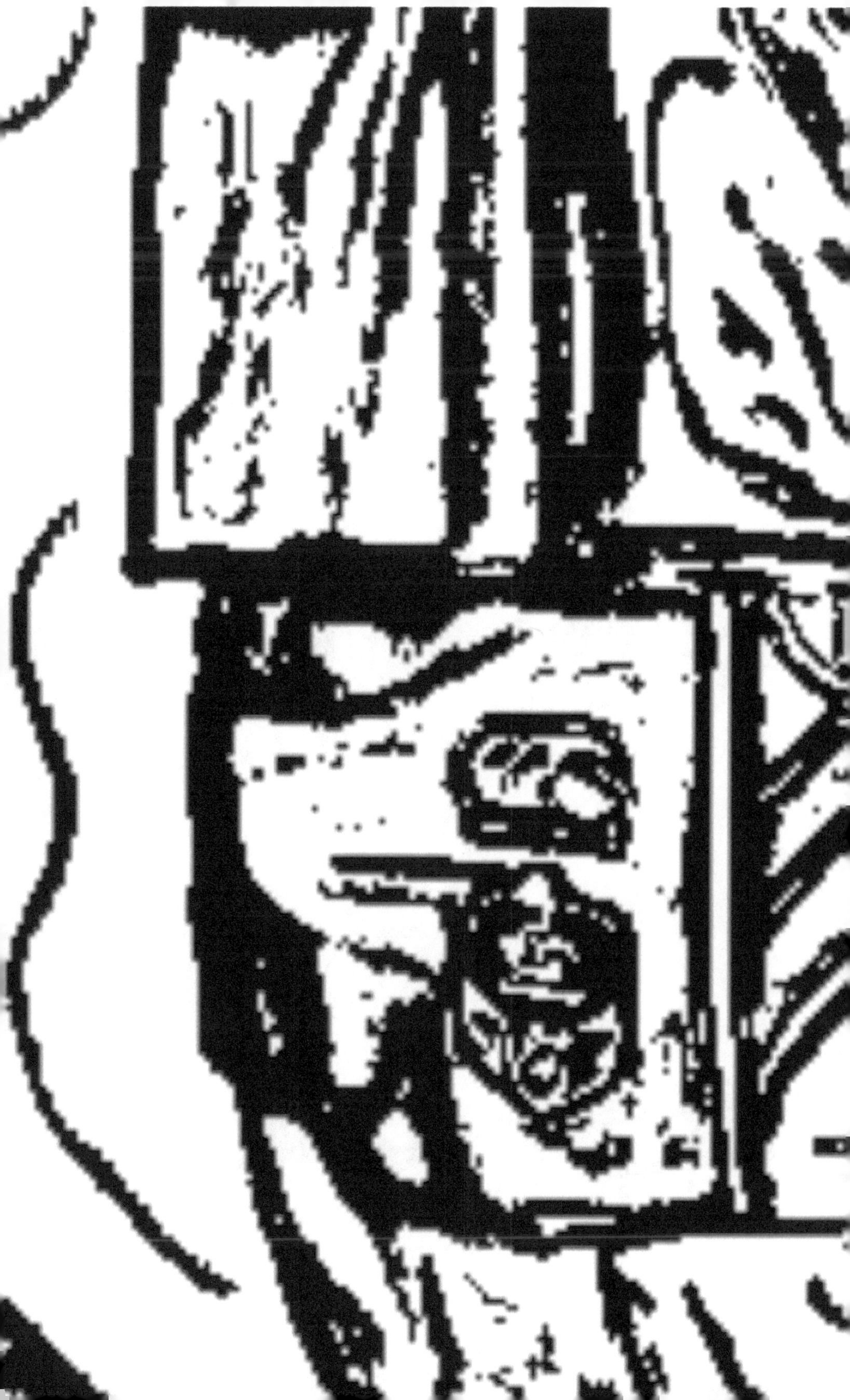

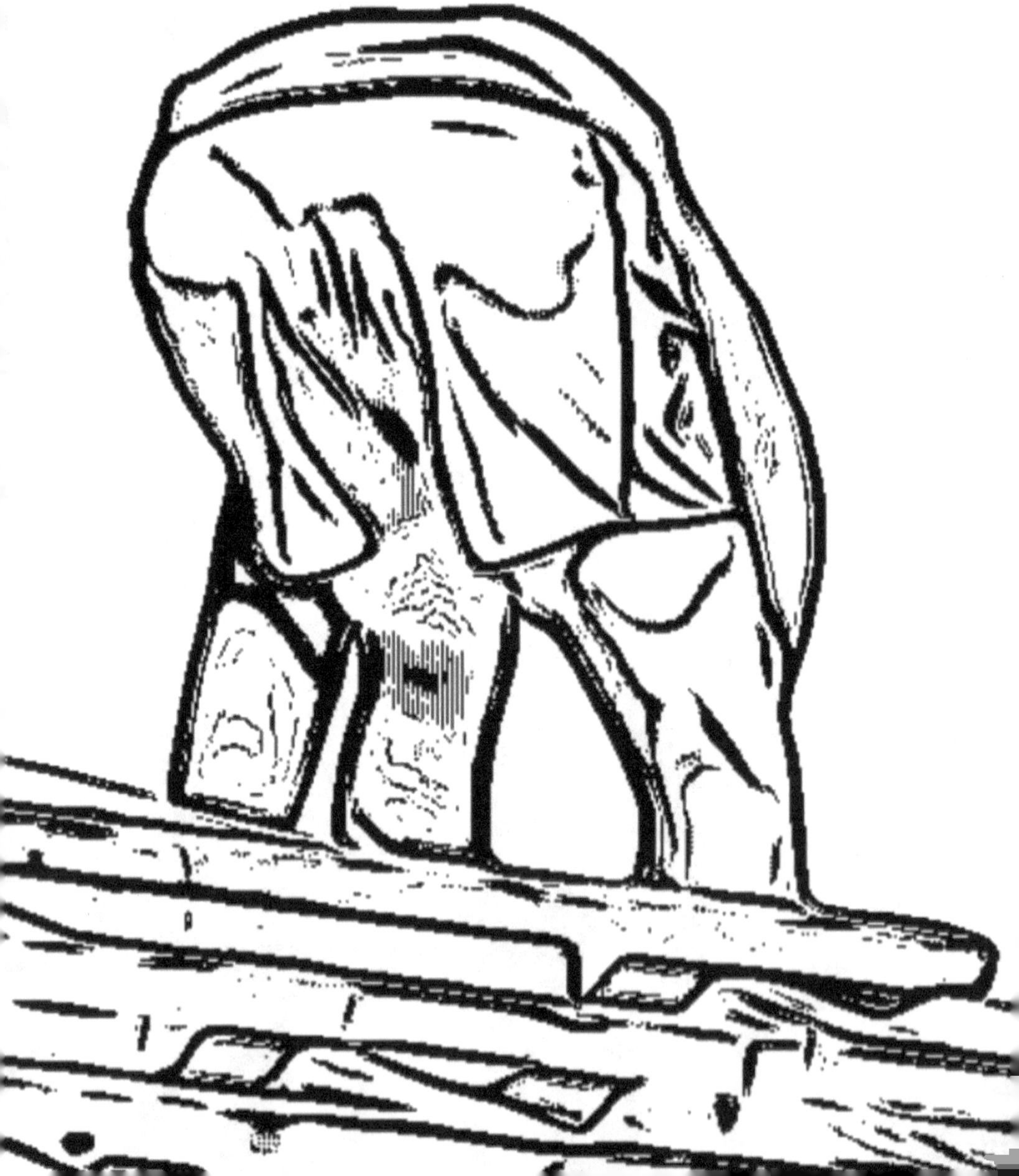

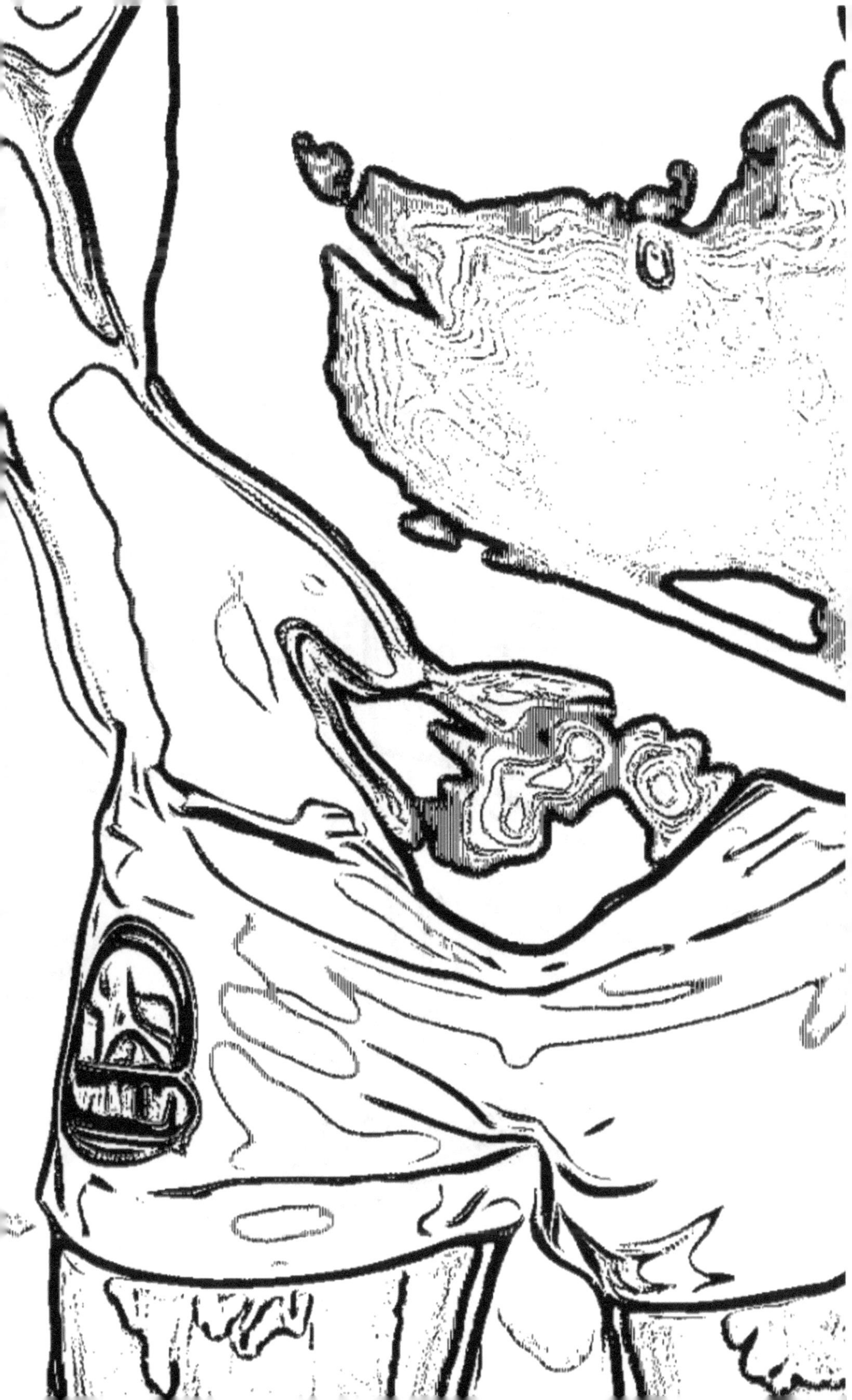

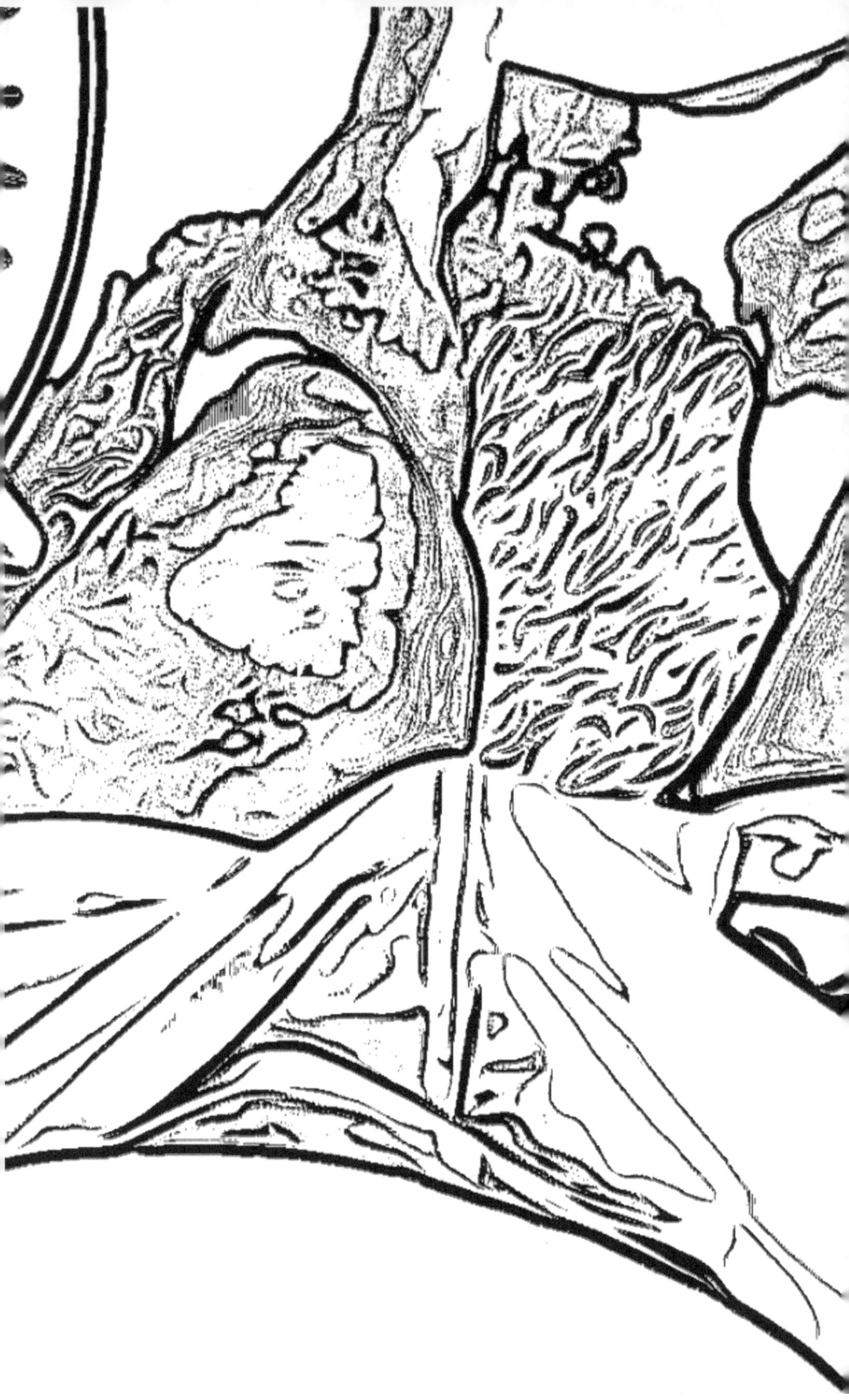

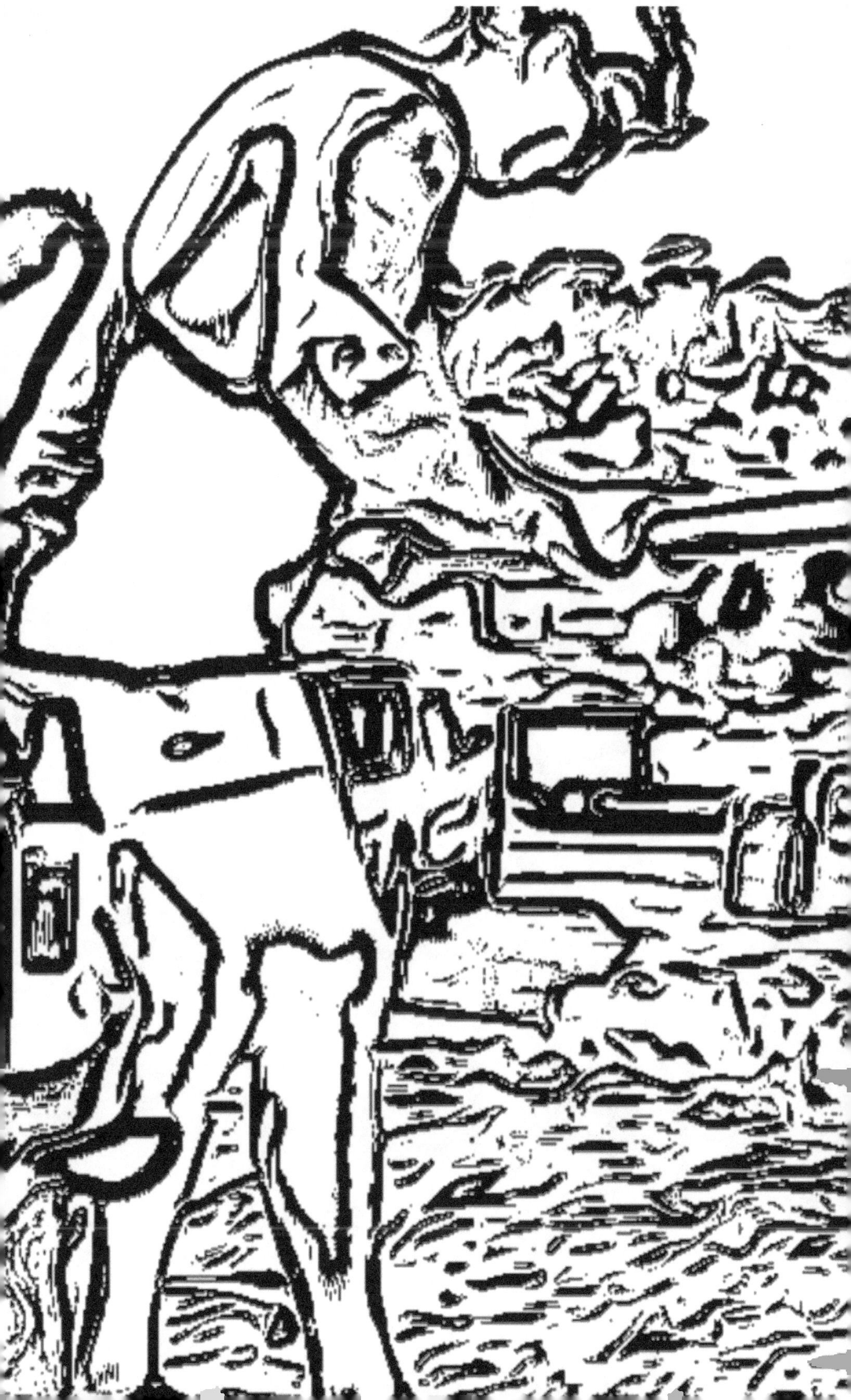

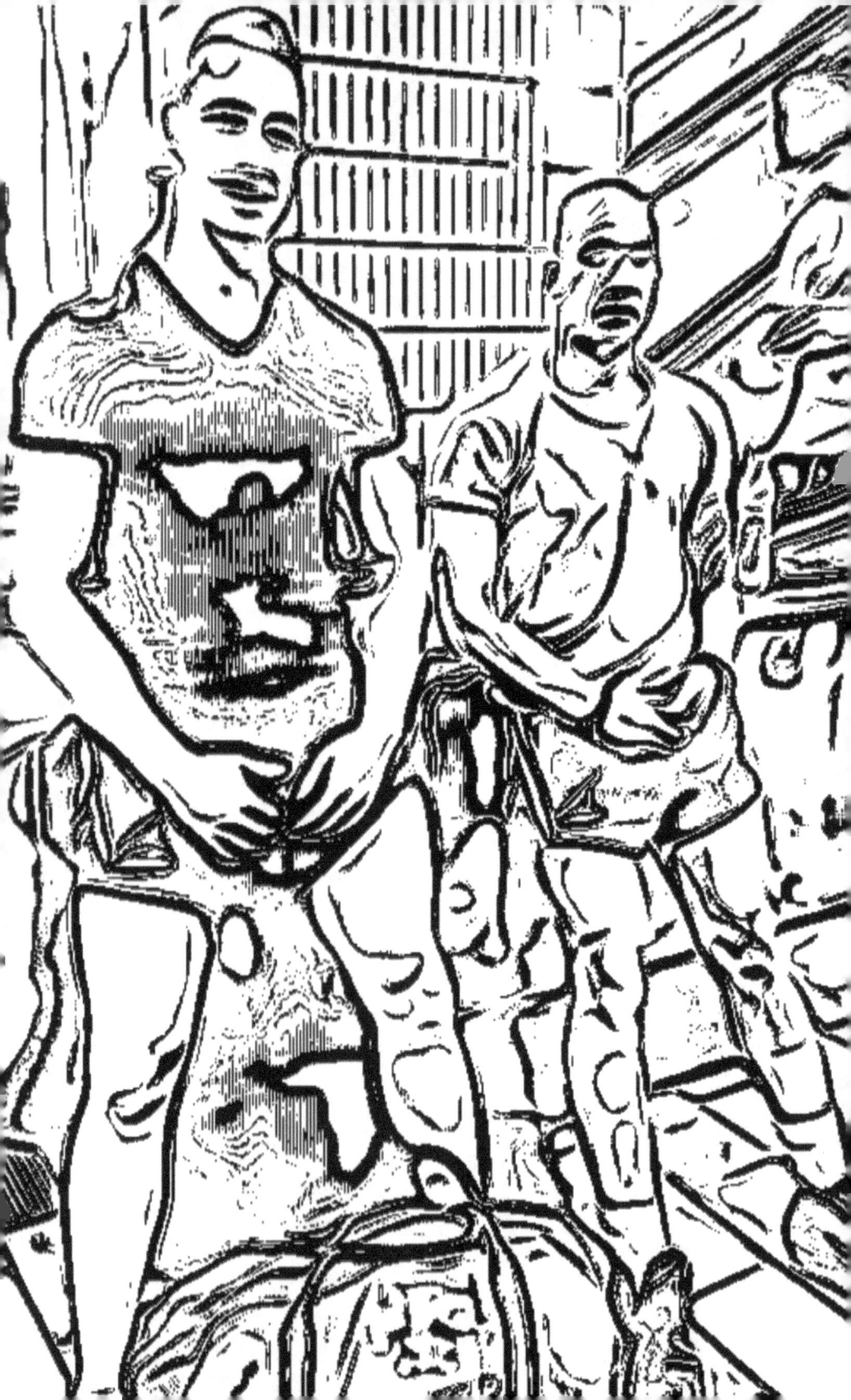

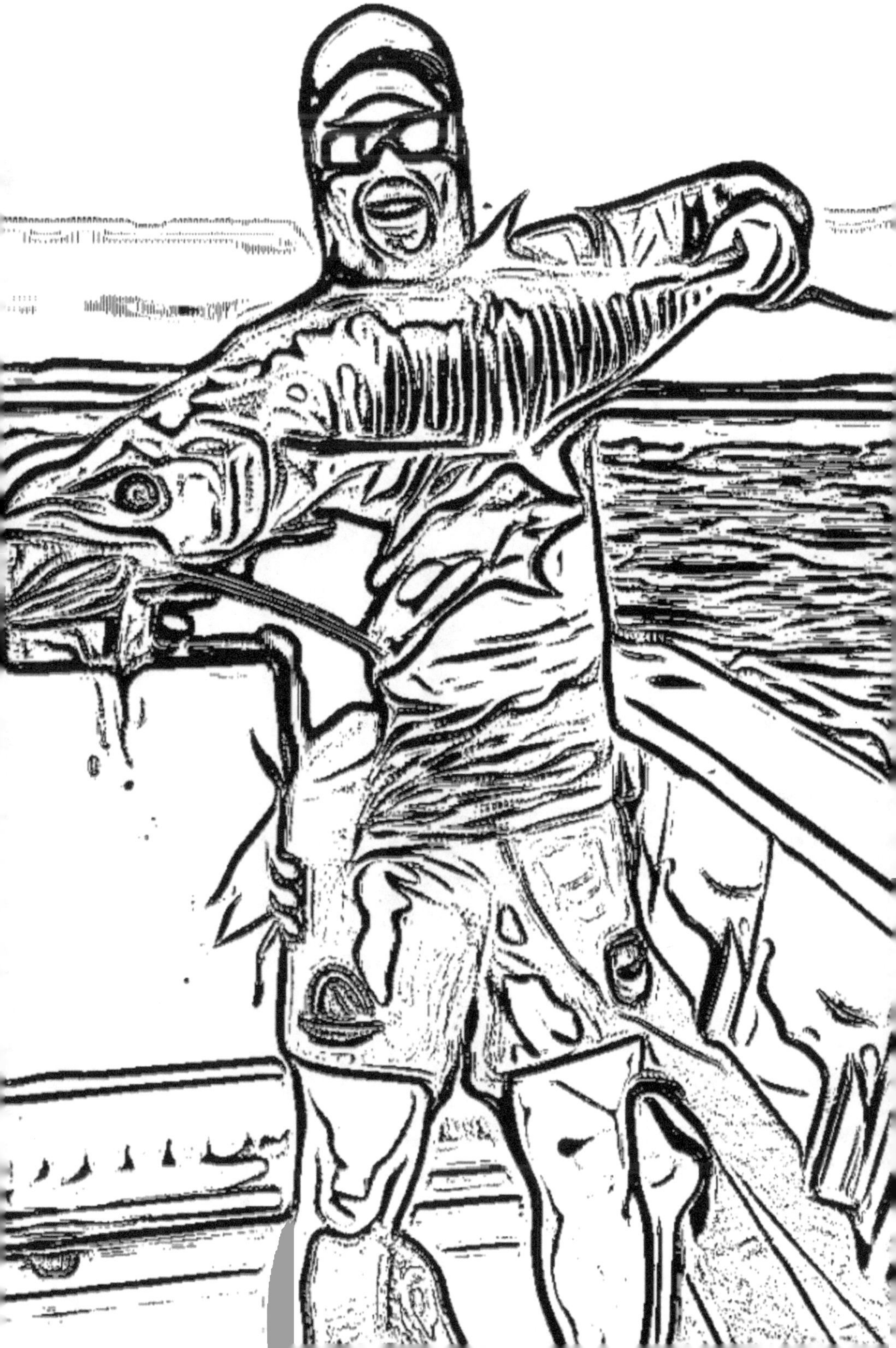

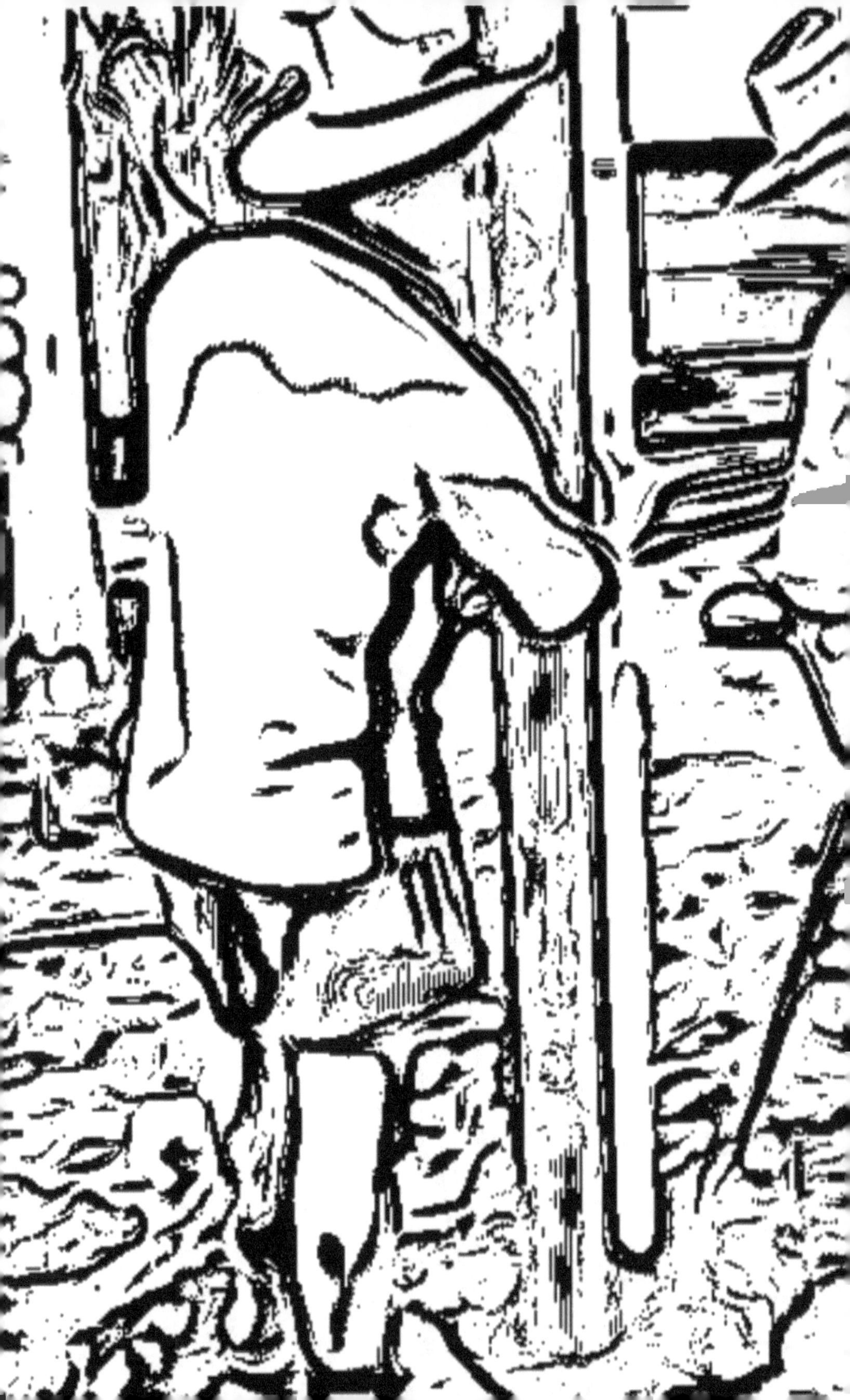

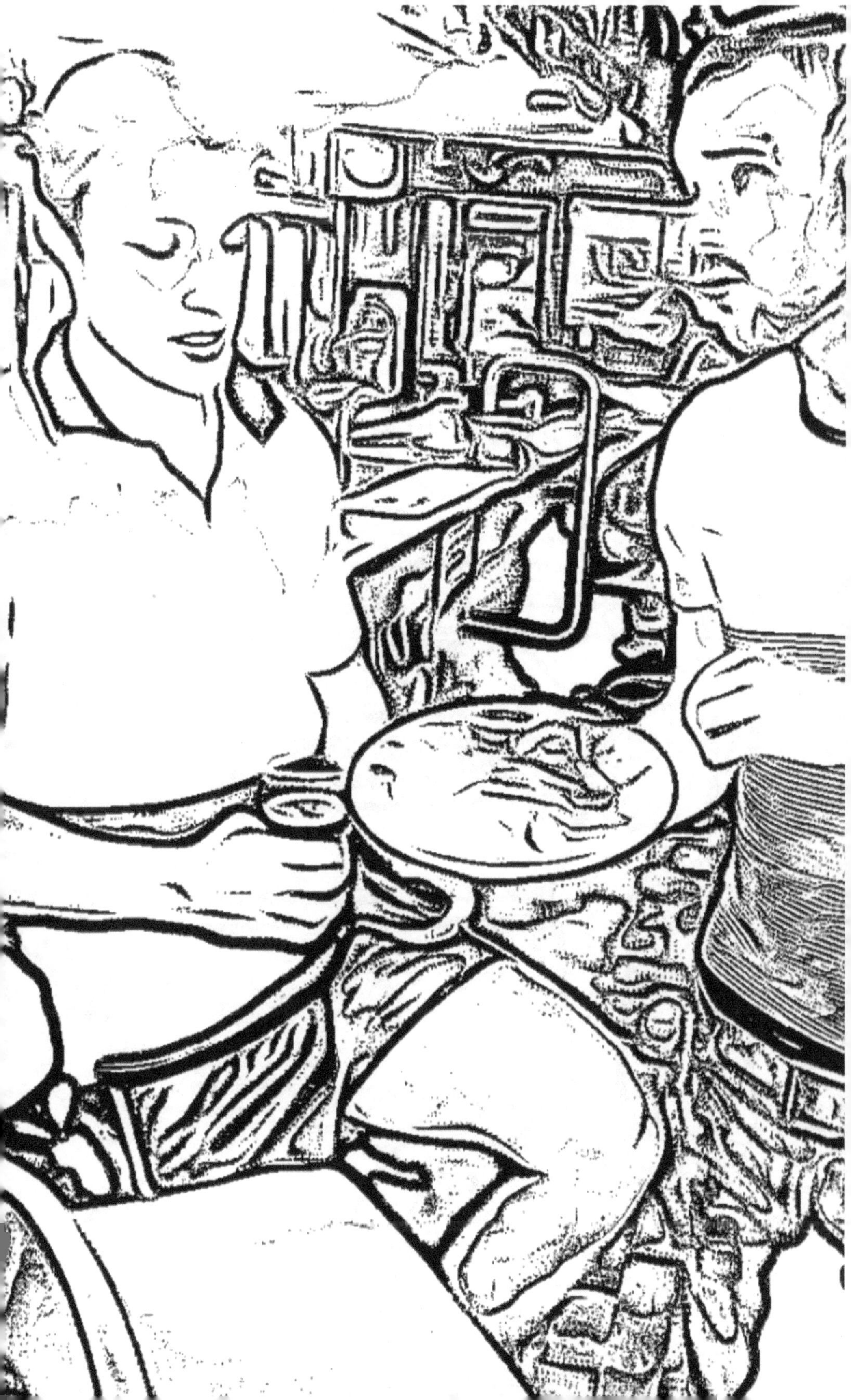

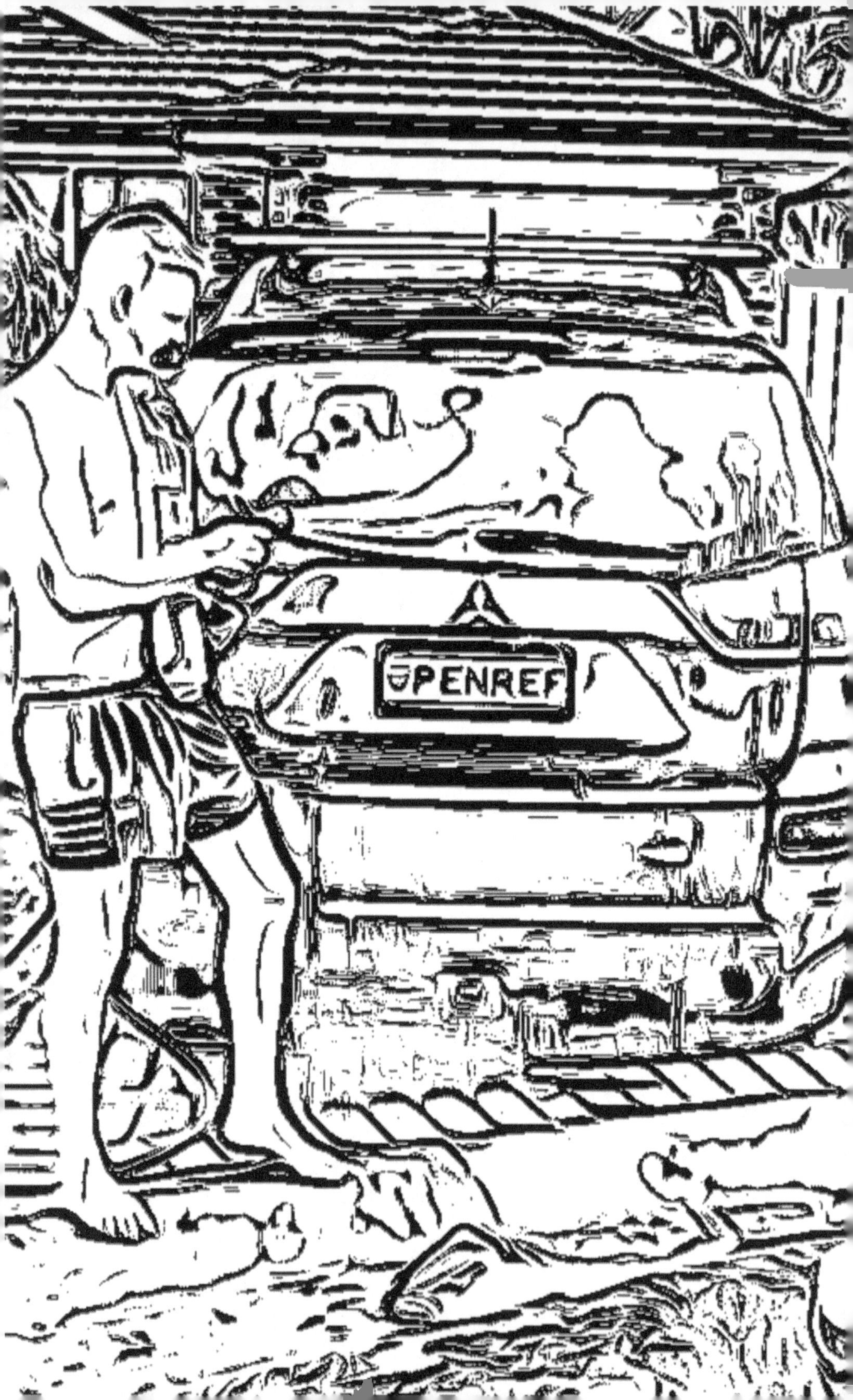
PENREF

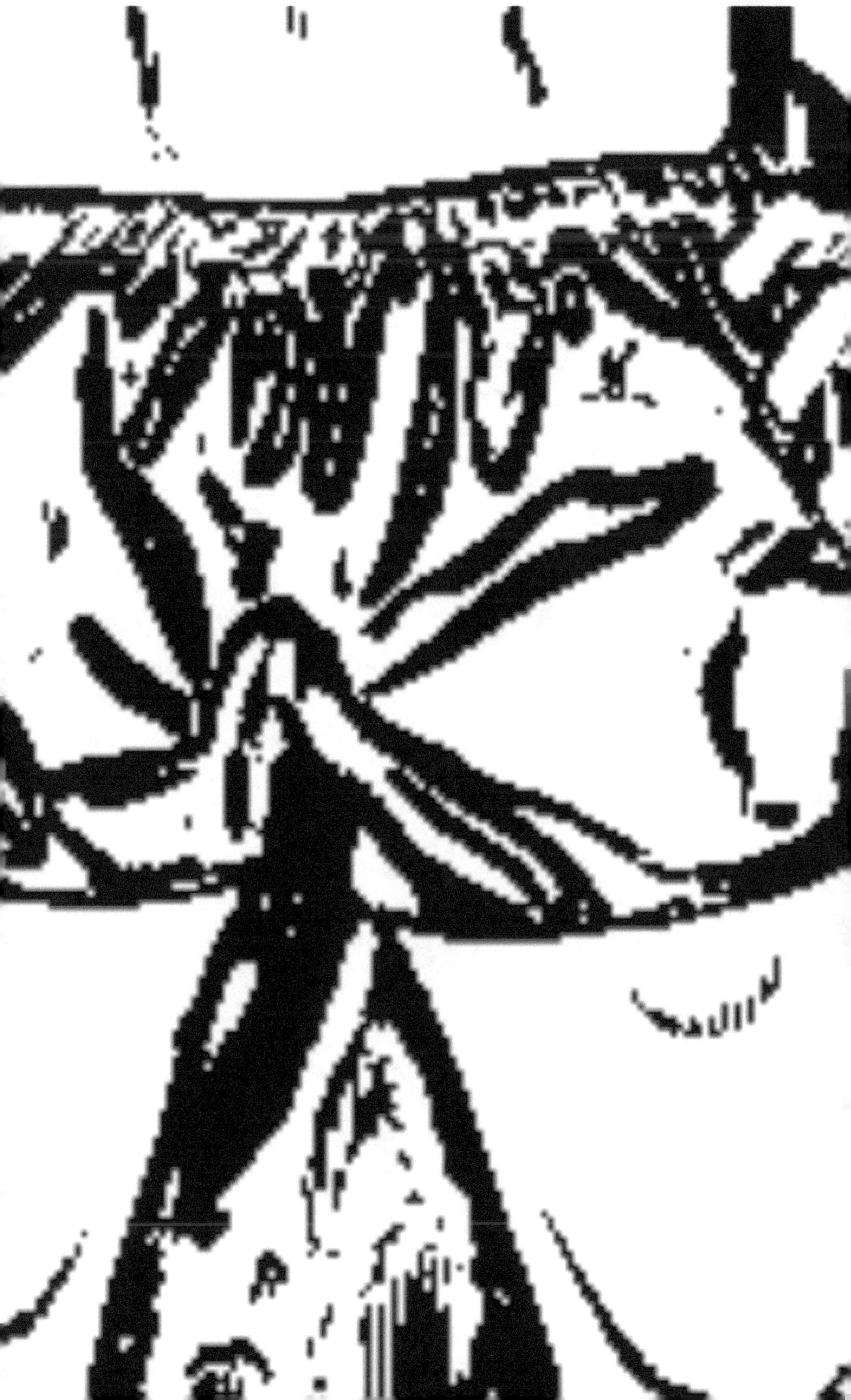

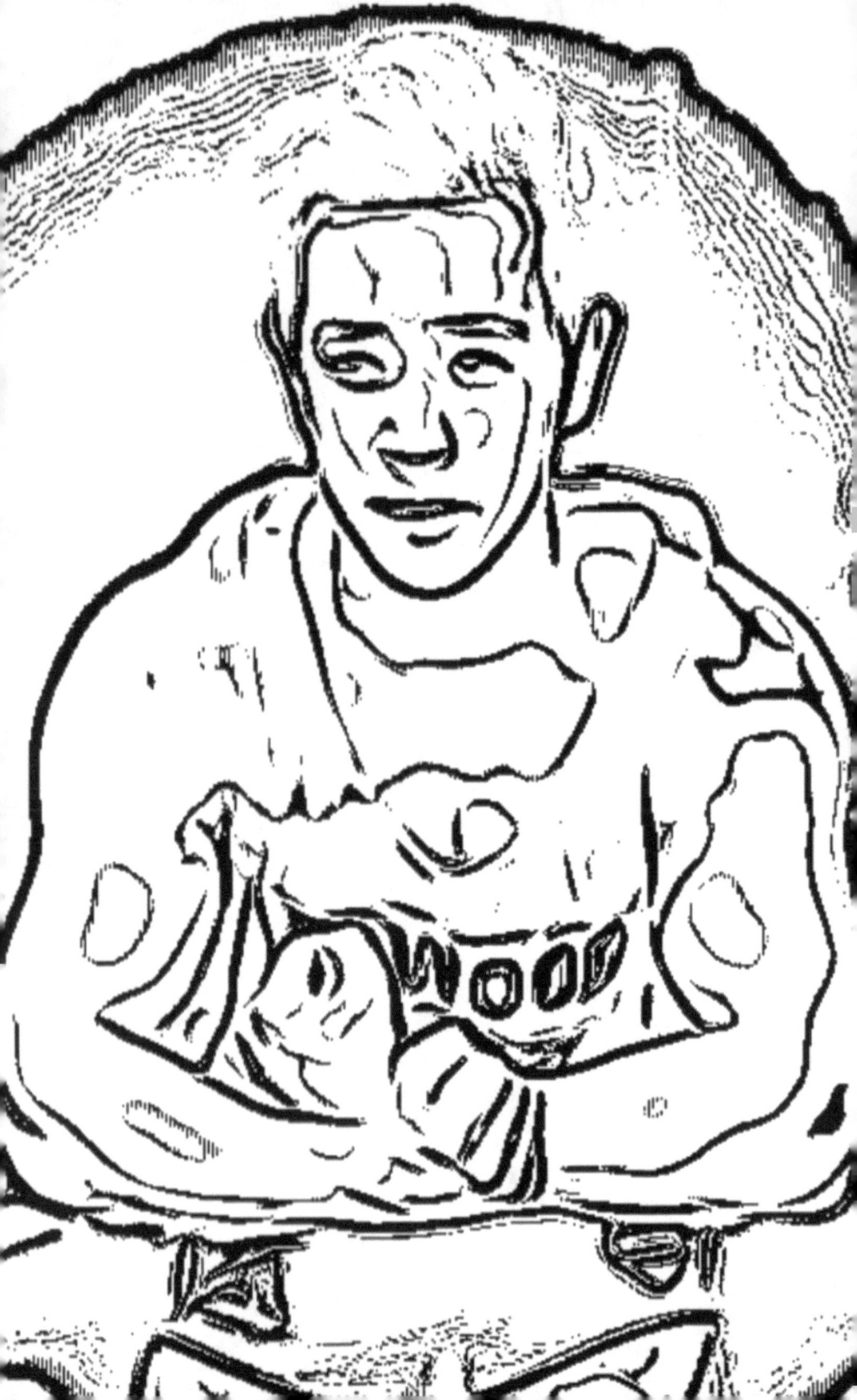
Wood

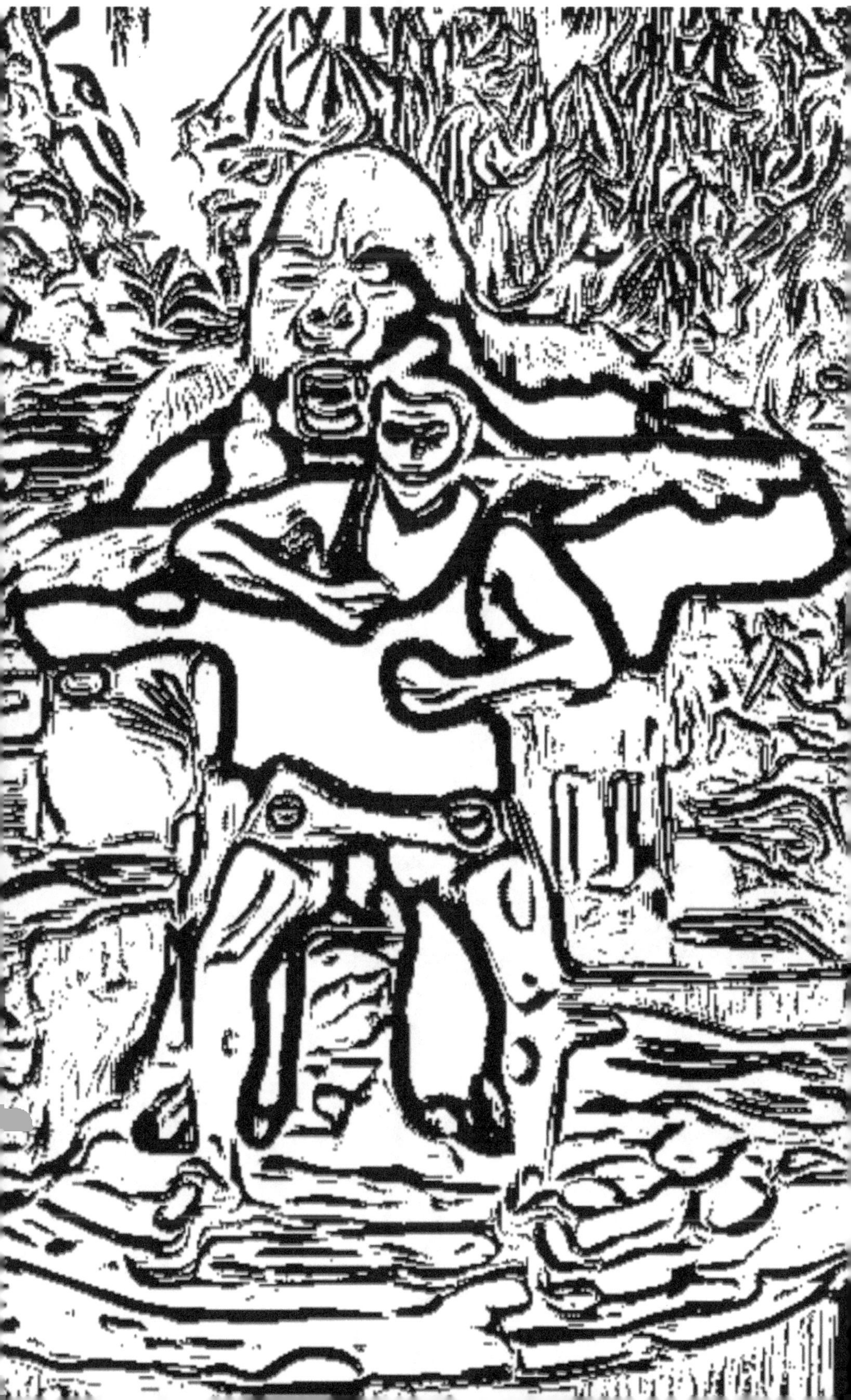

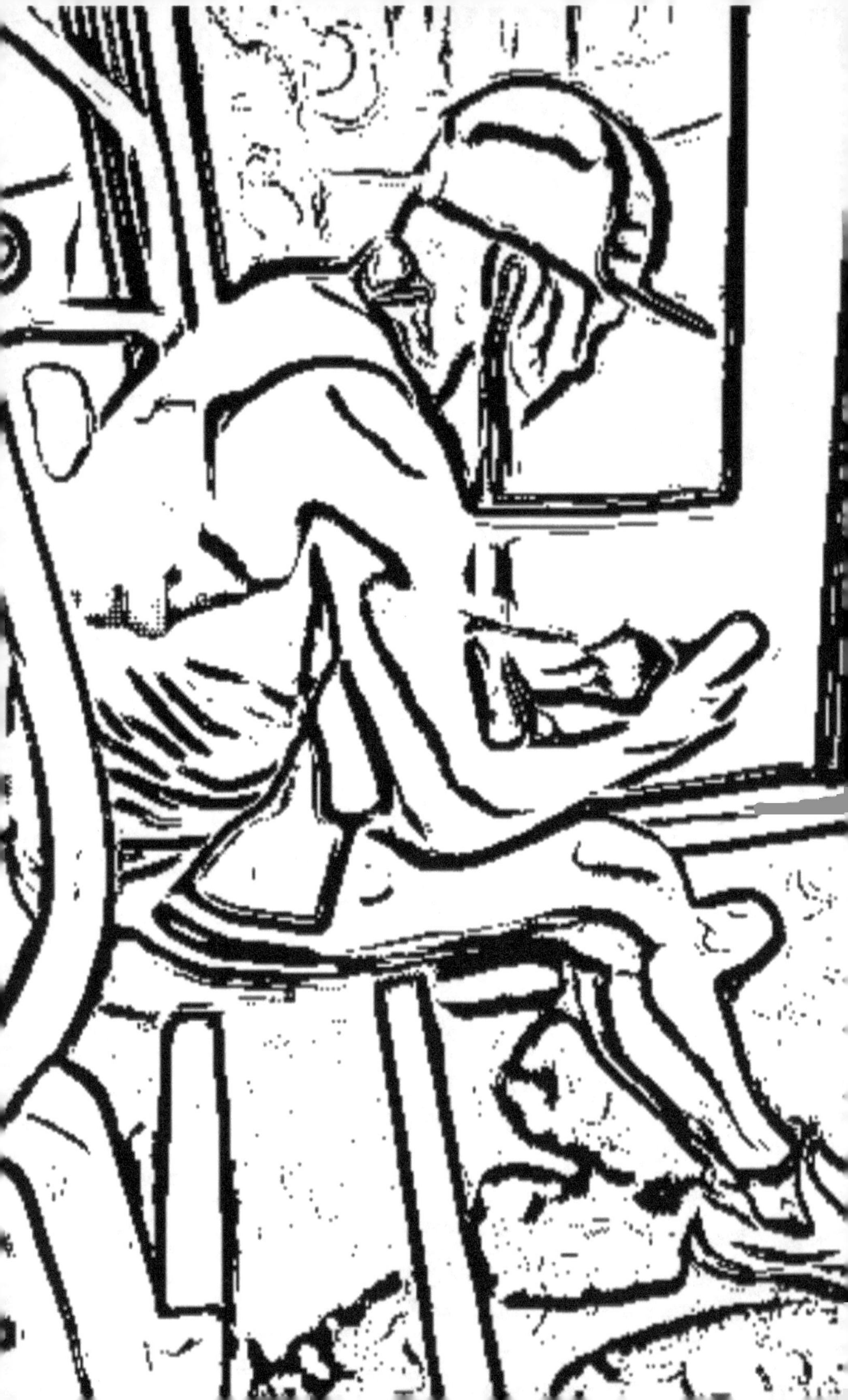

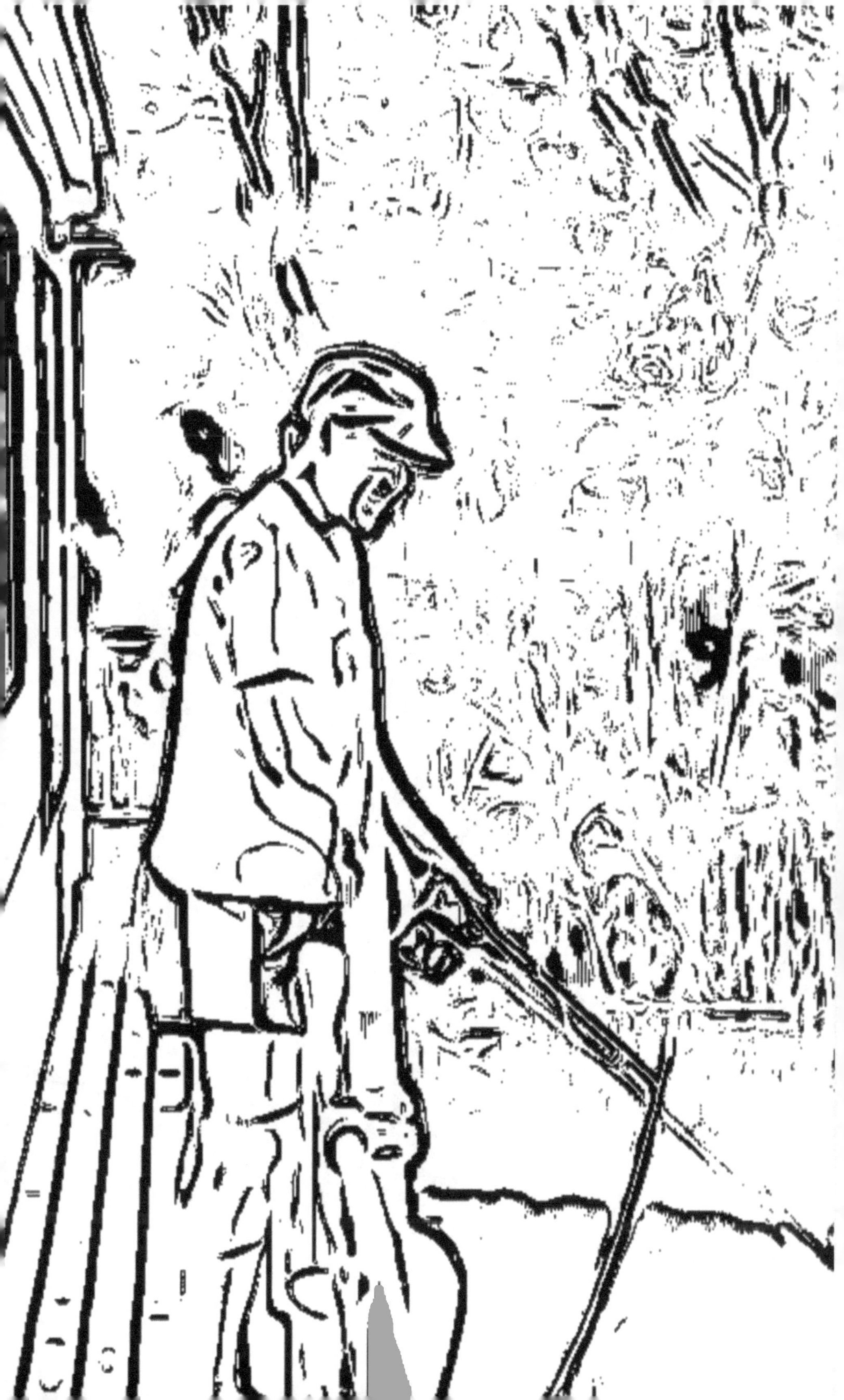

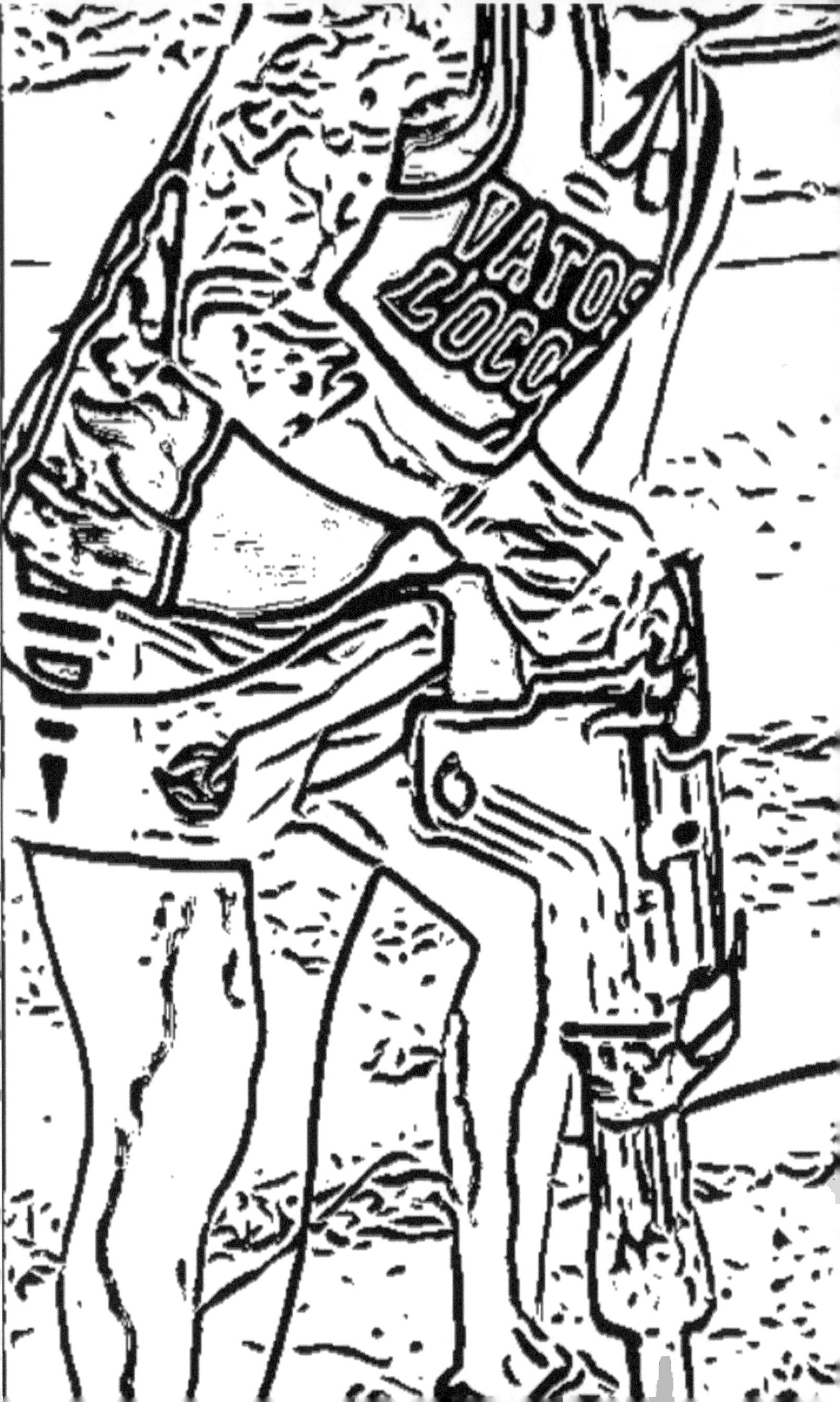
VATOS
LOCO

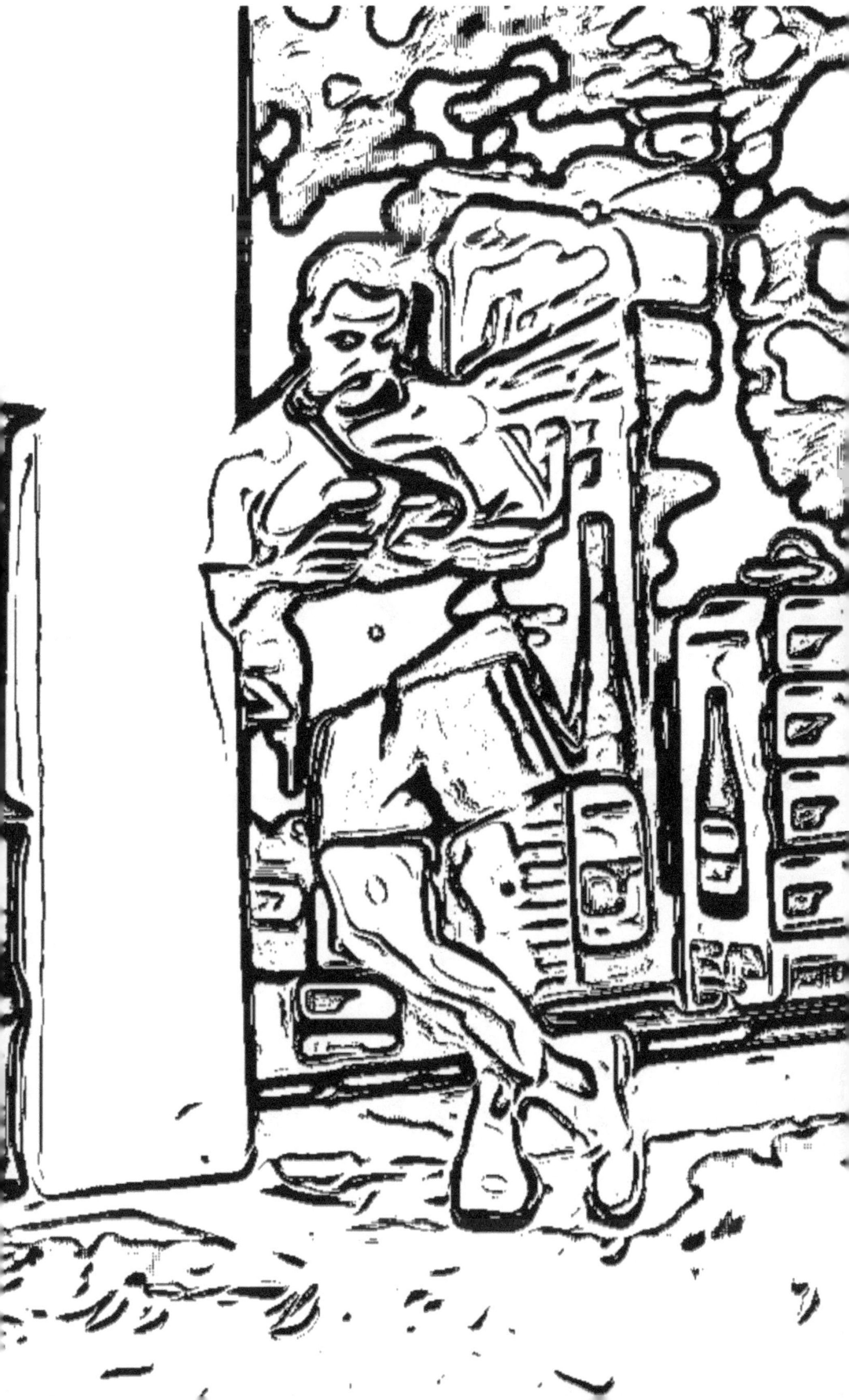

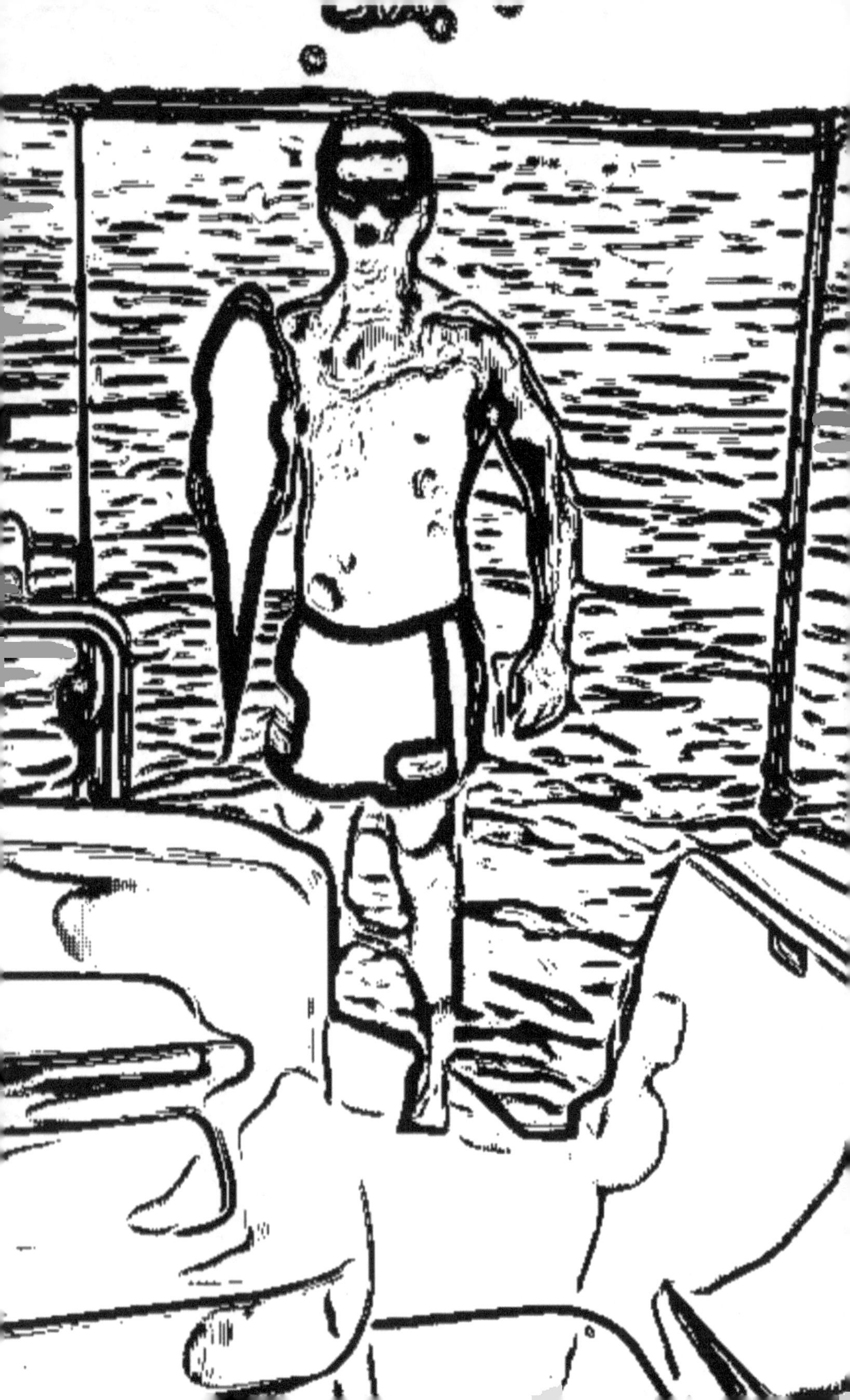

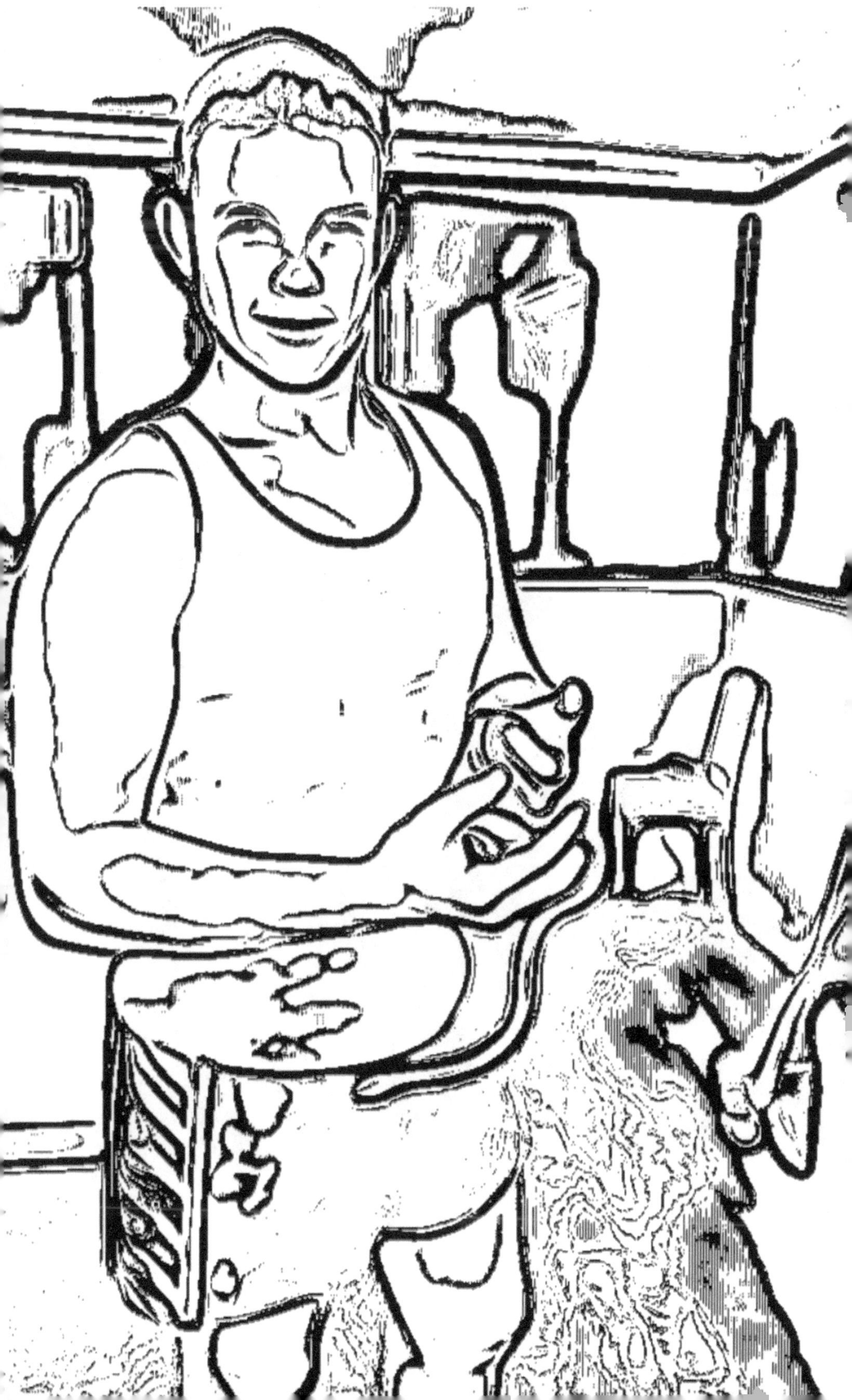

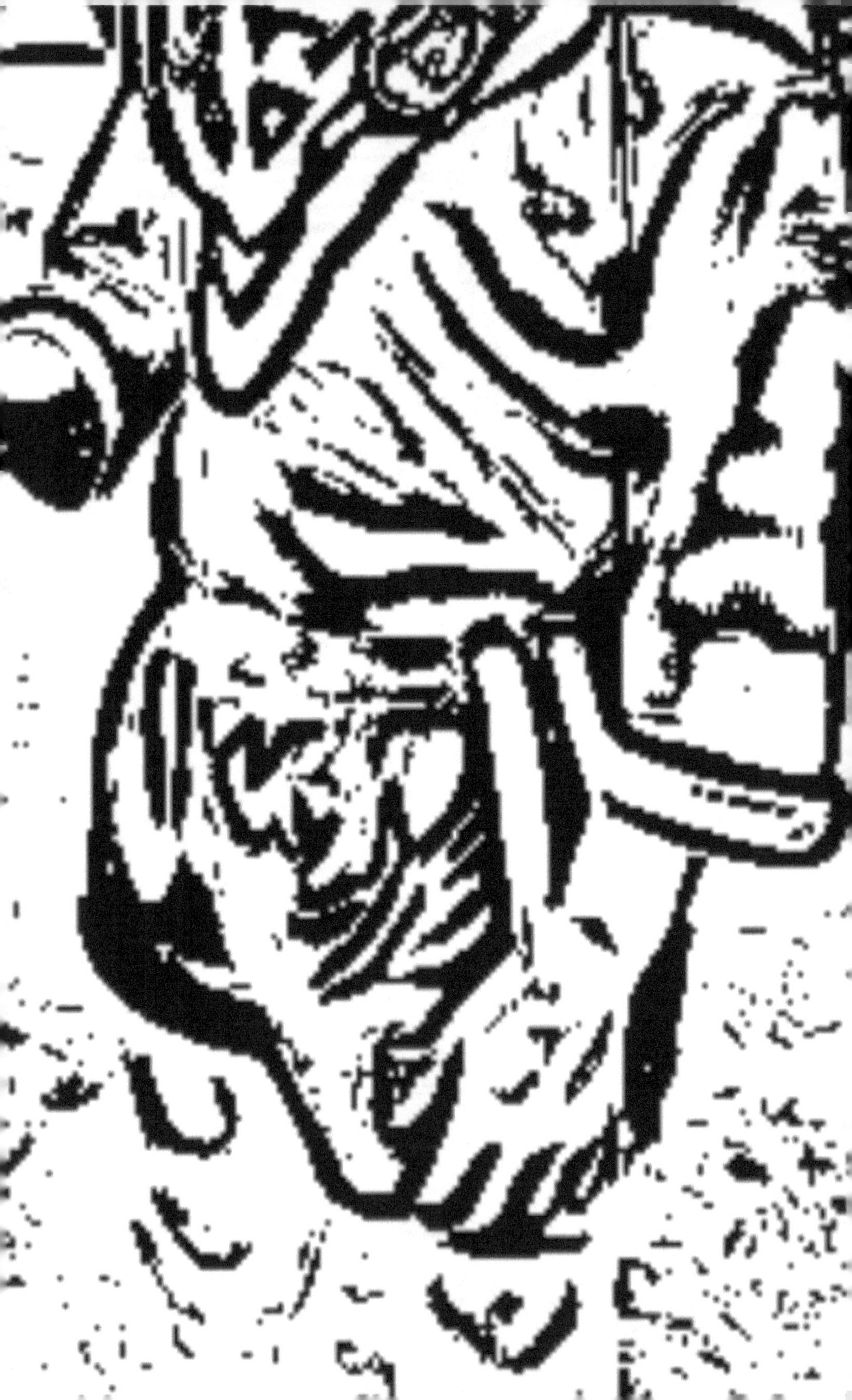

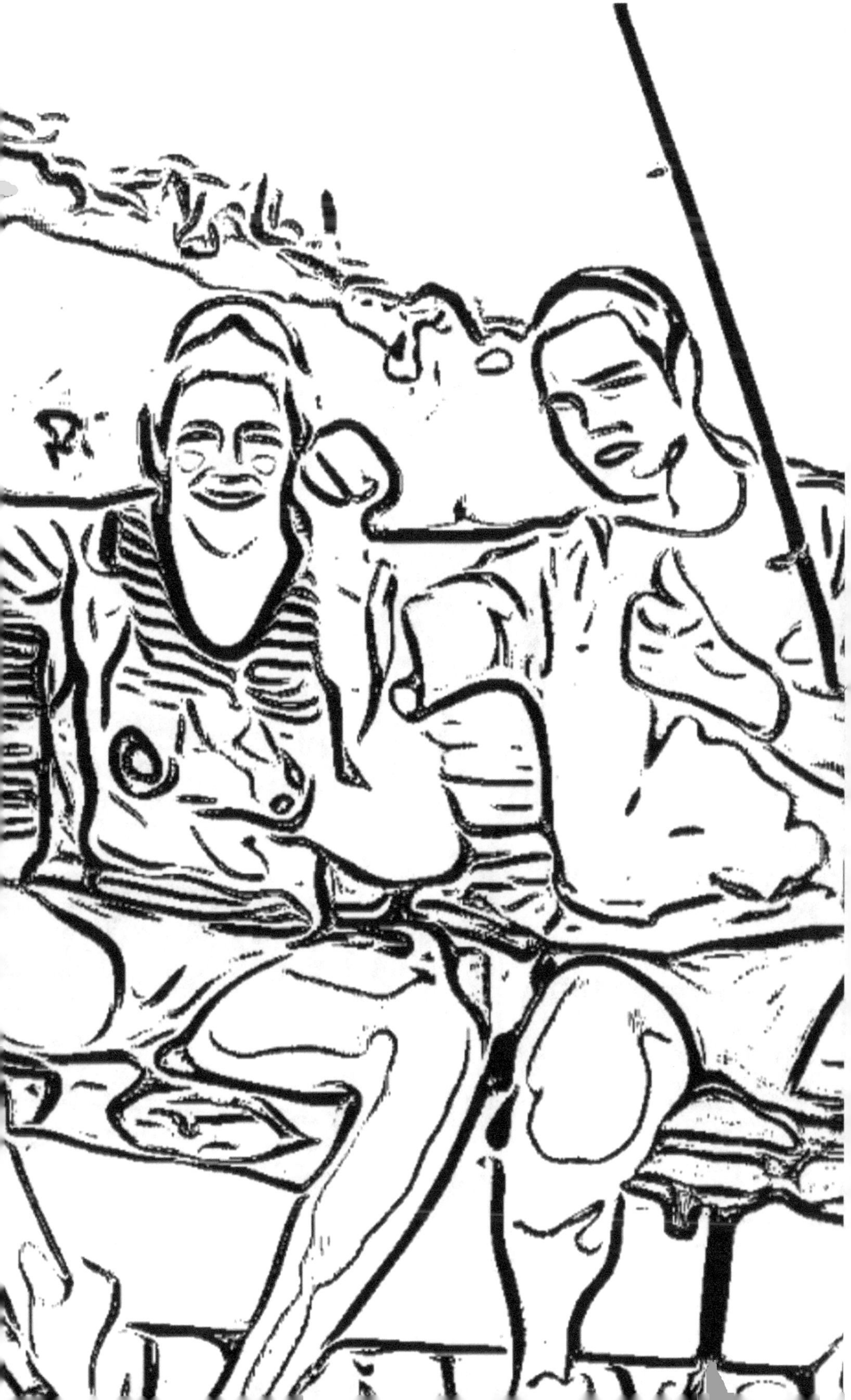

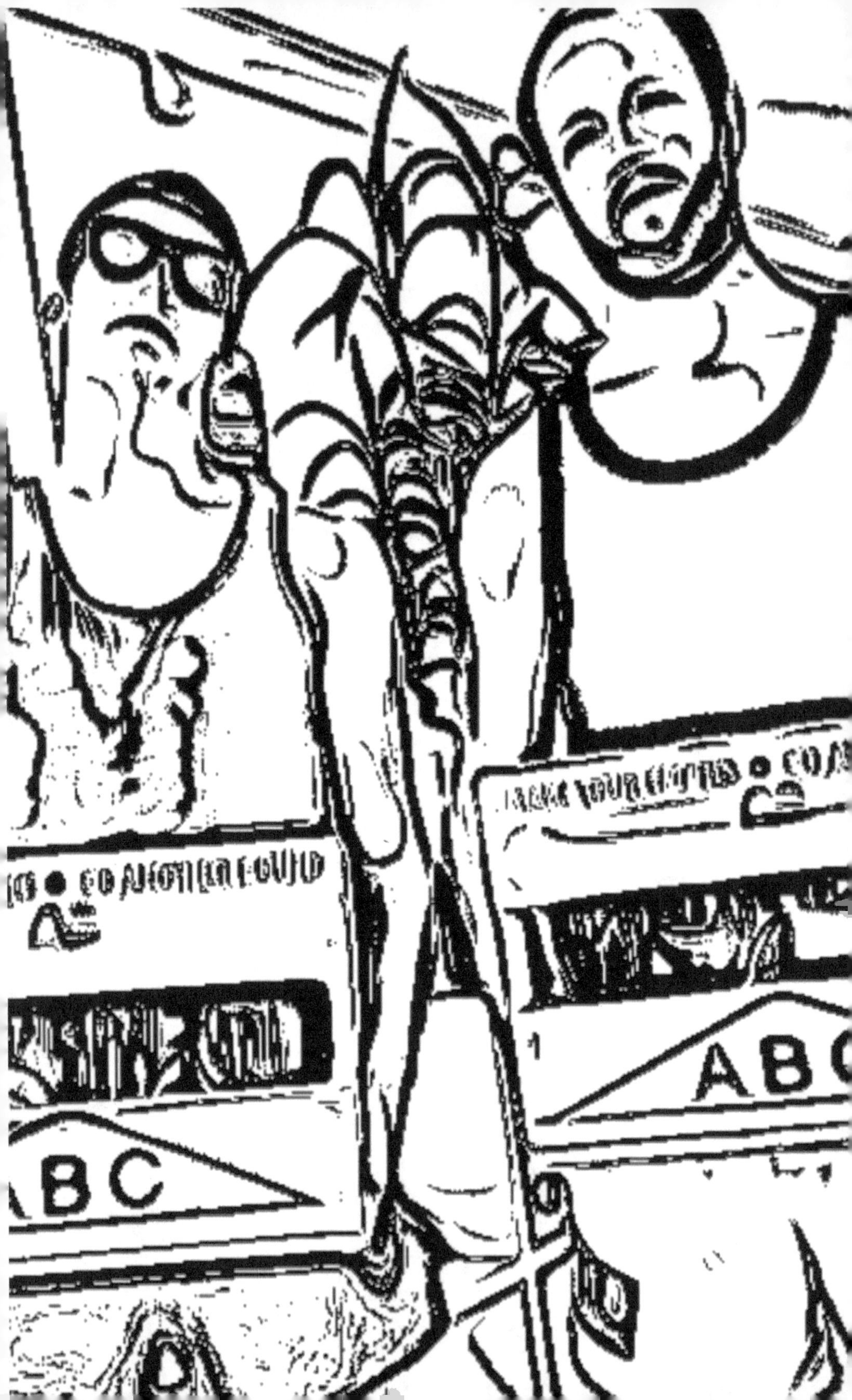
ABC

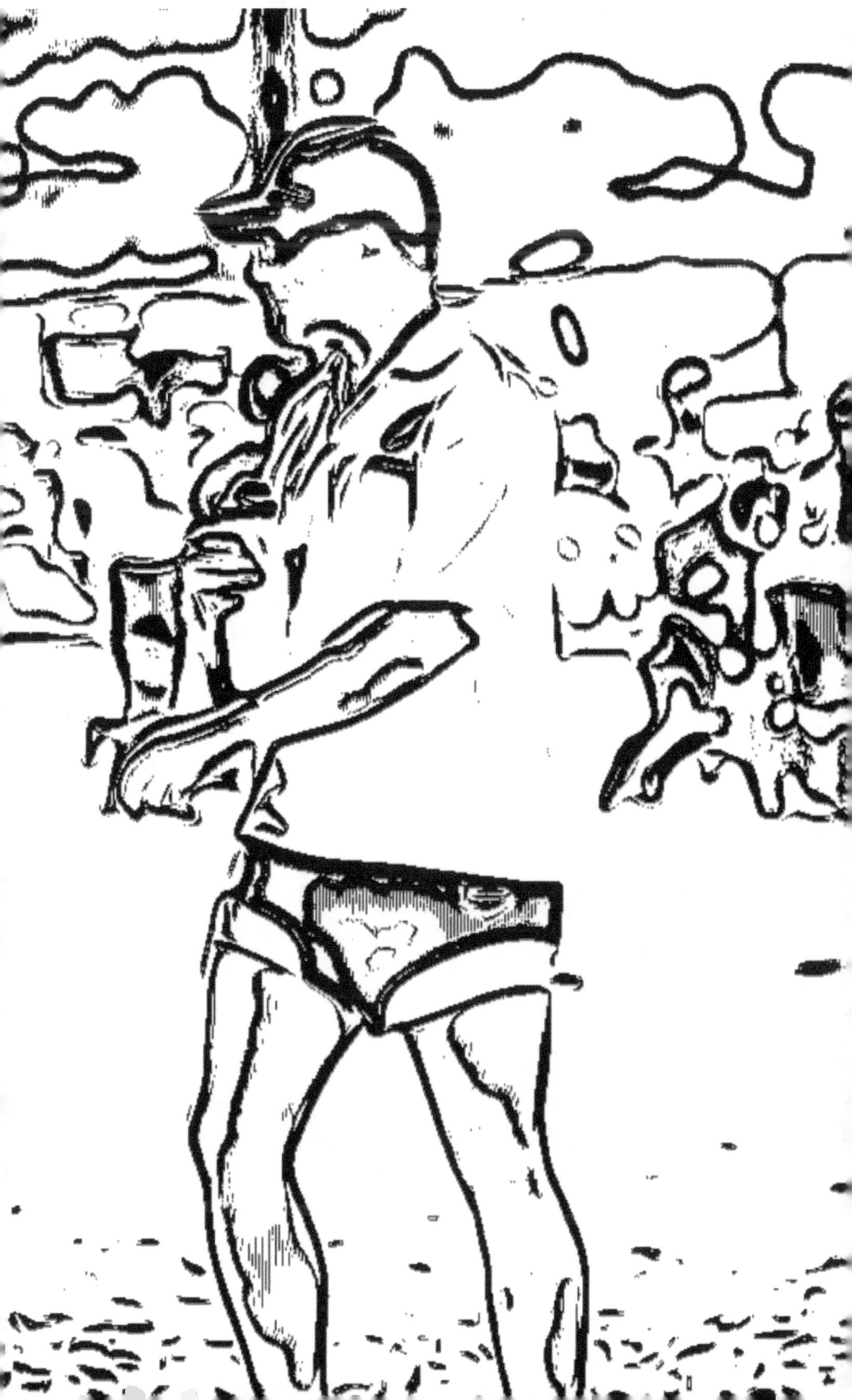

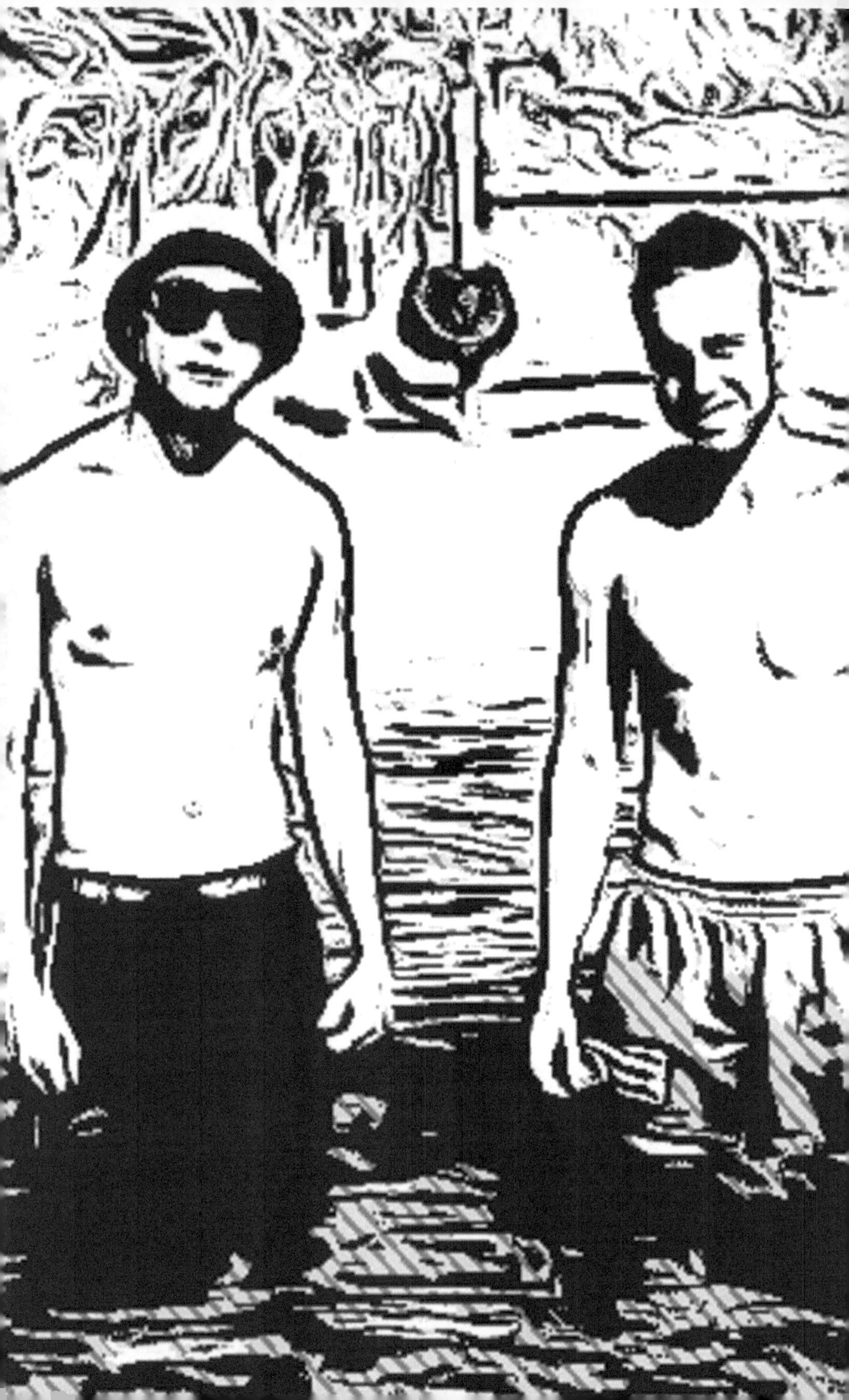

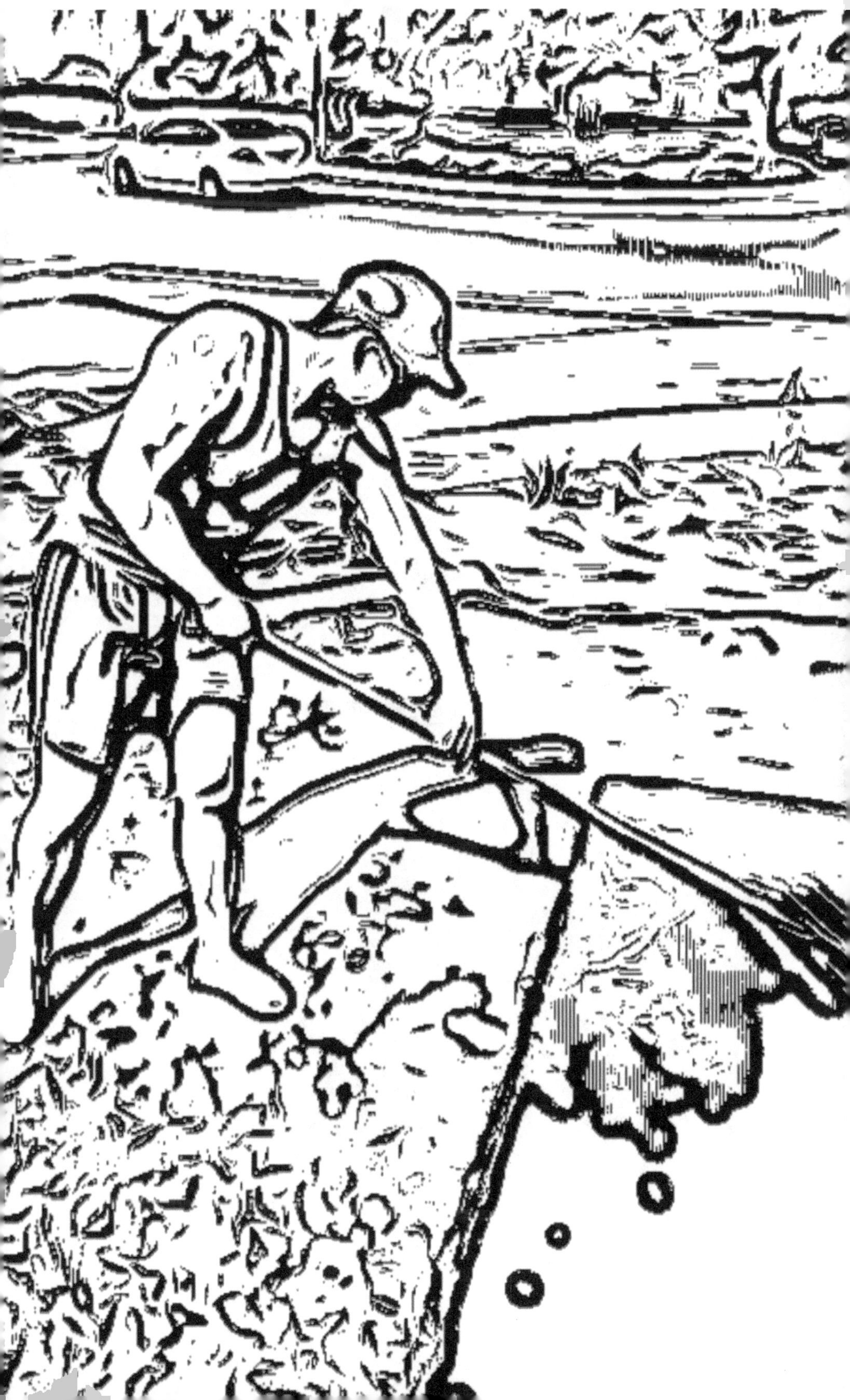

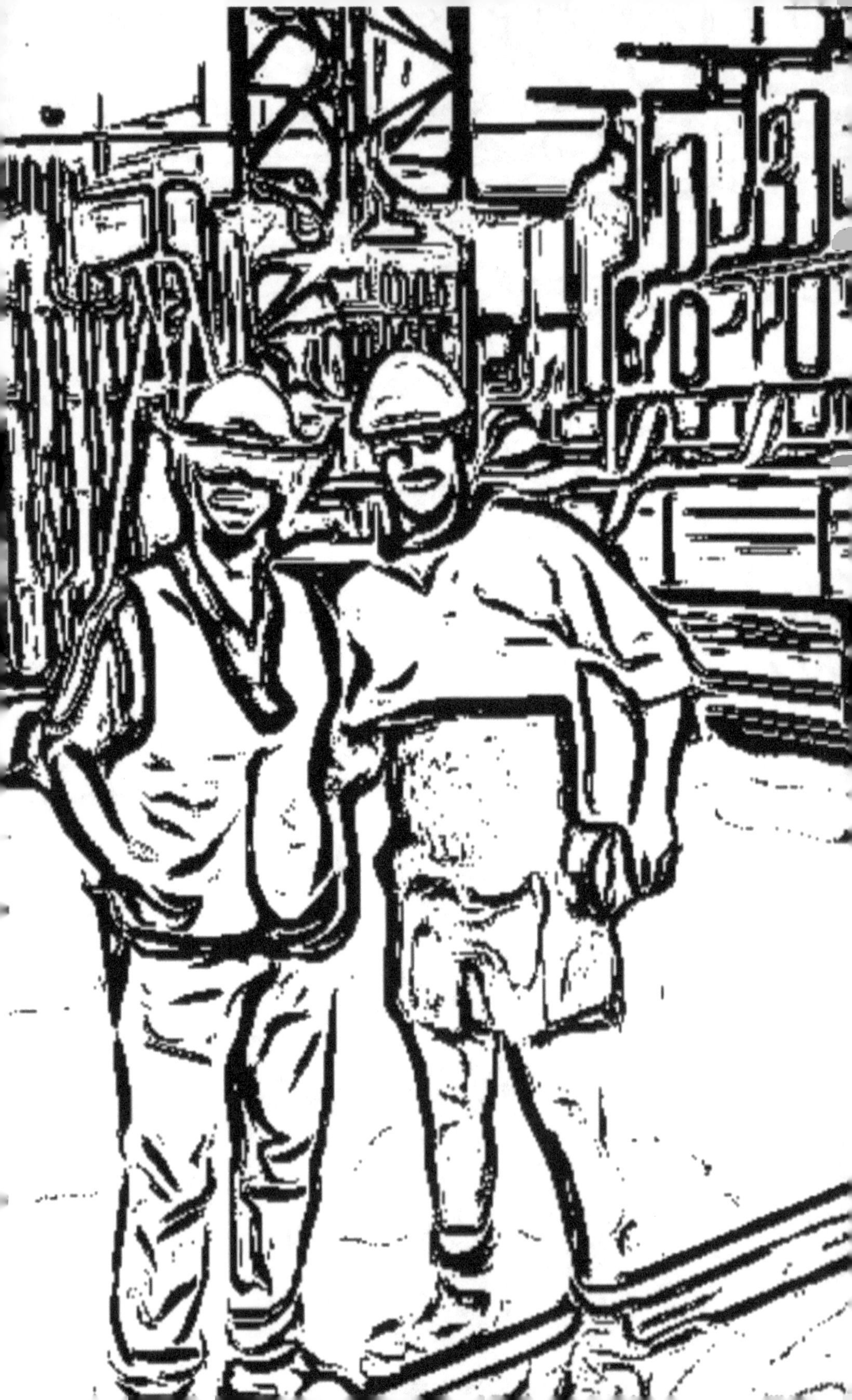

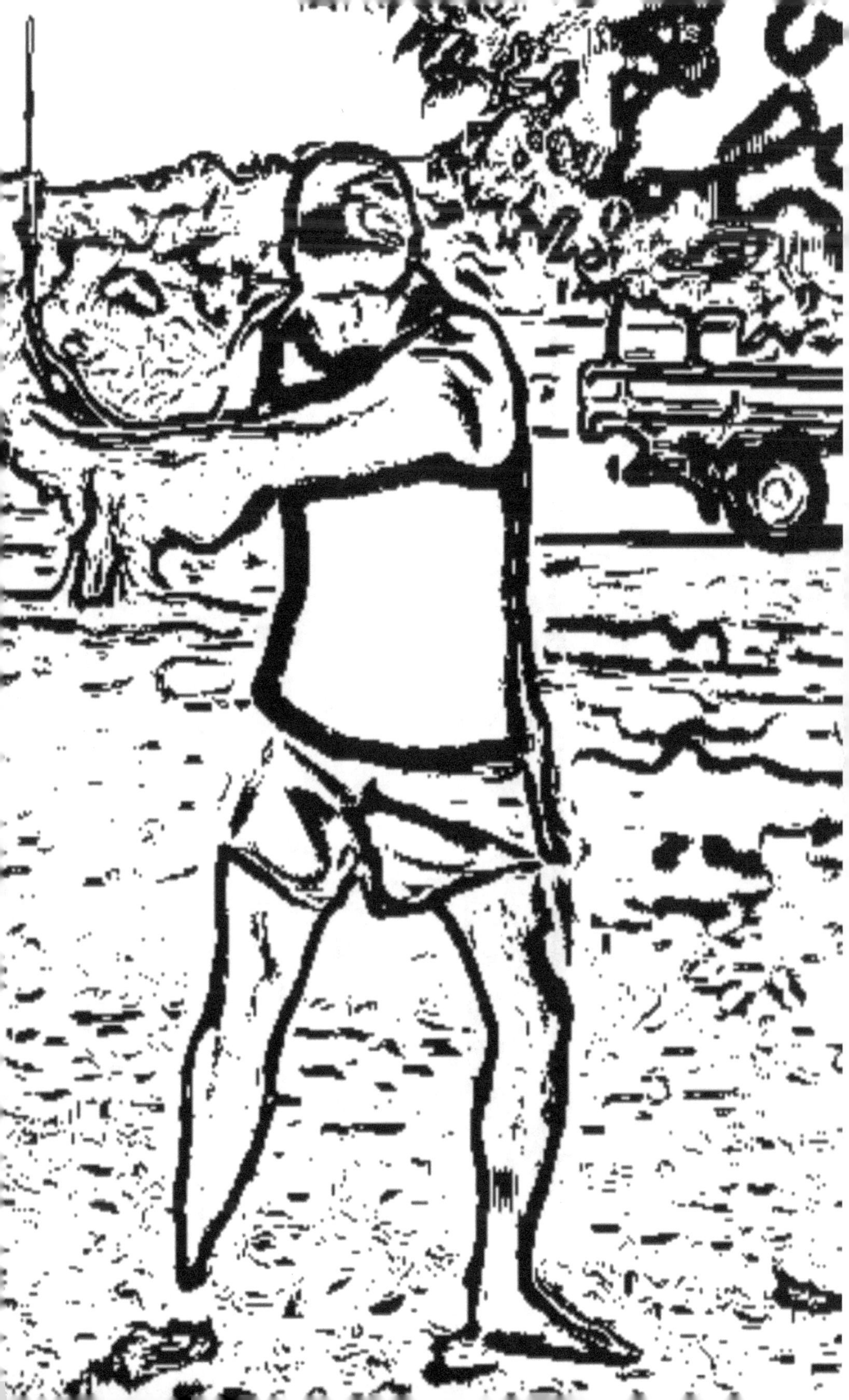

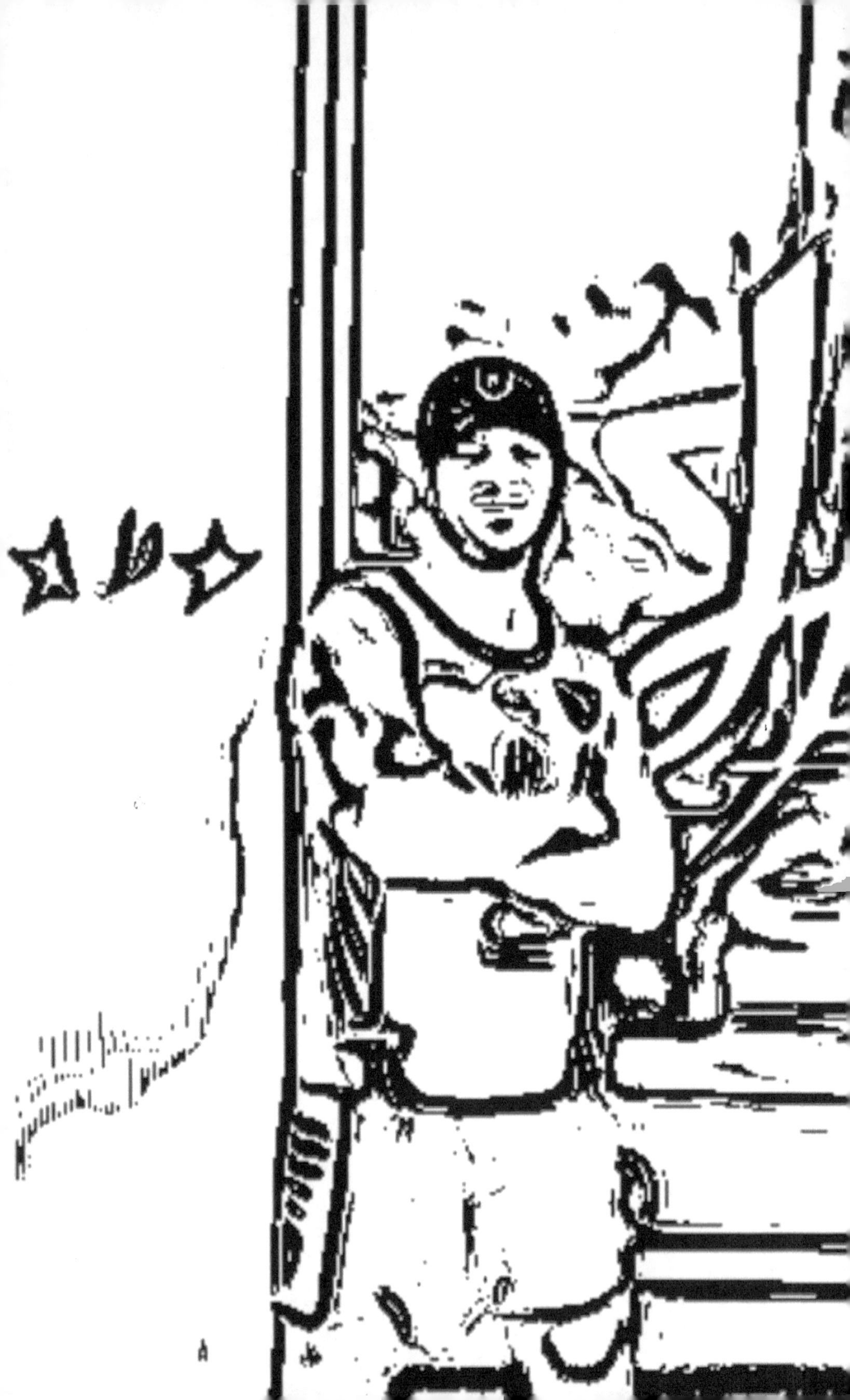

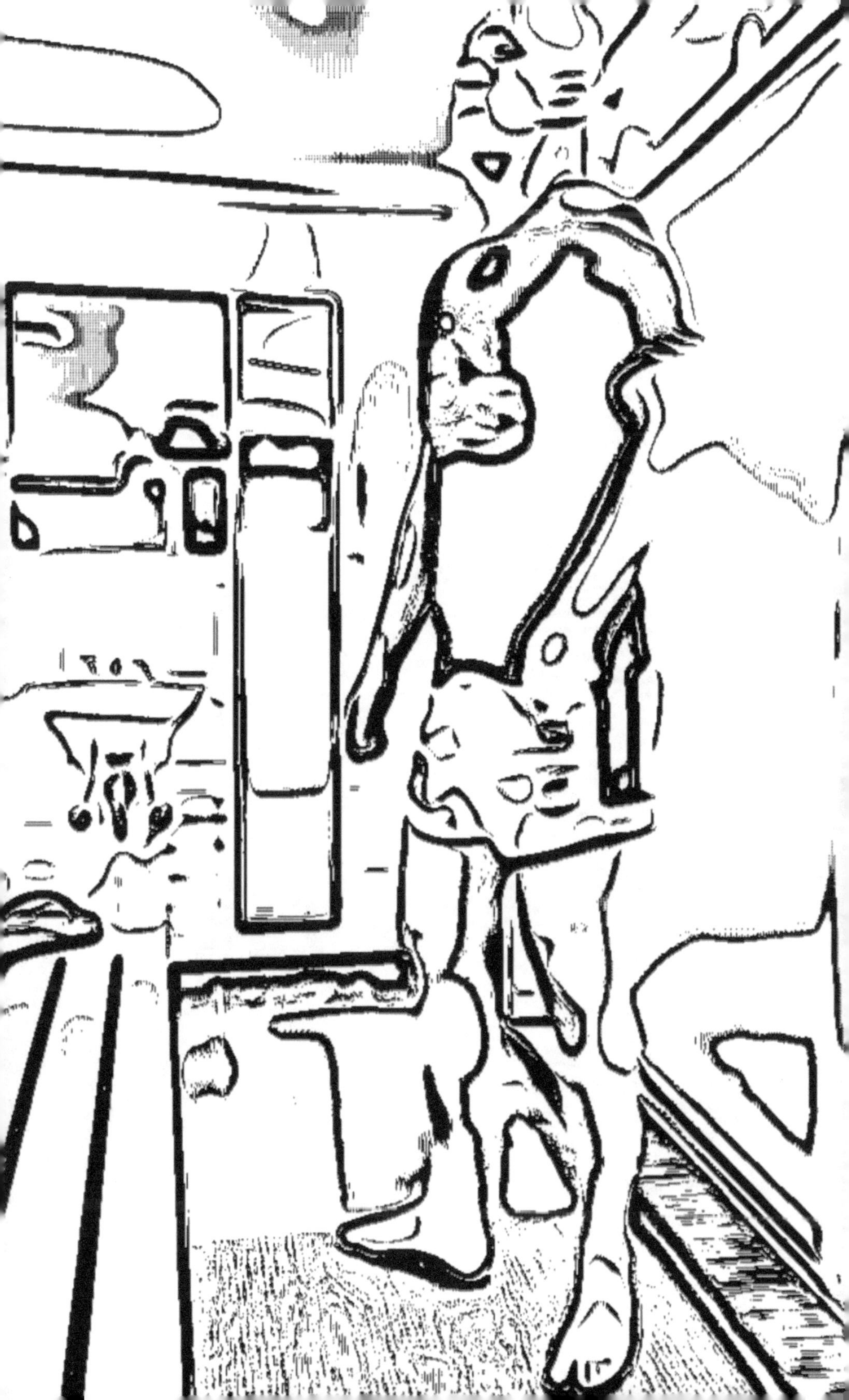

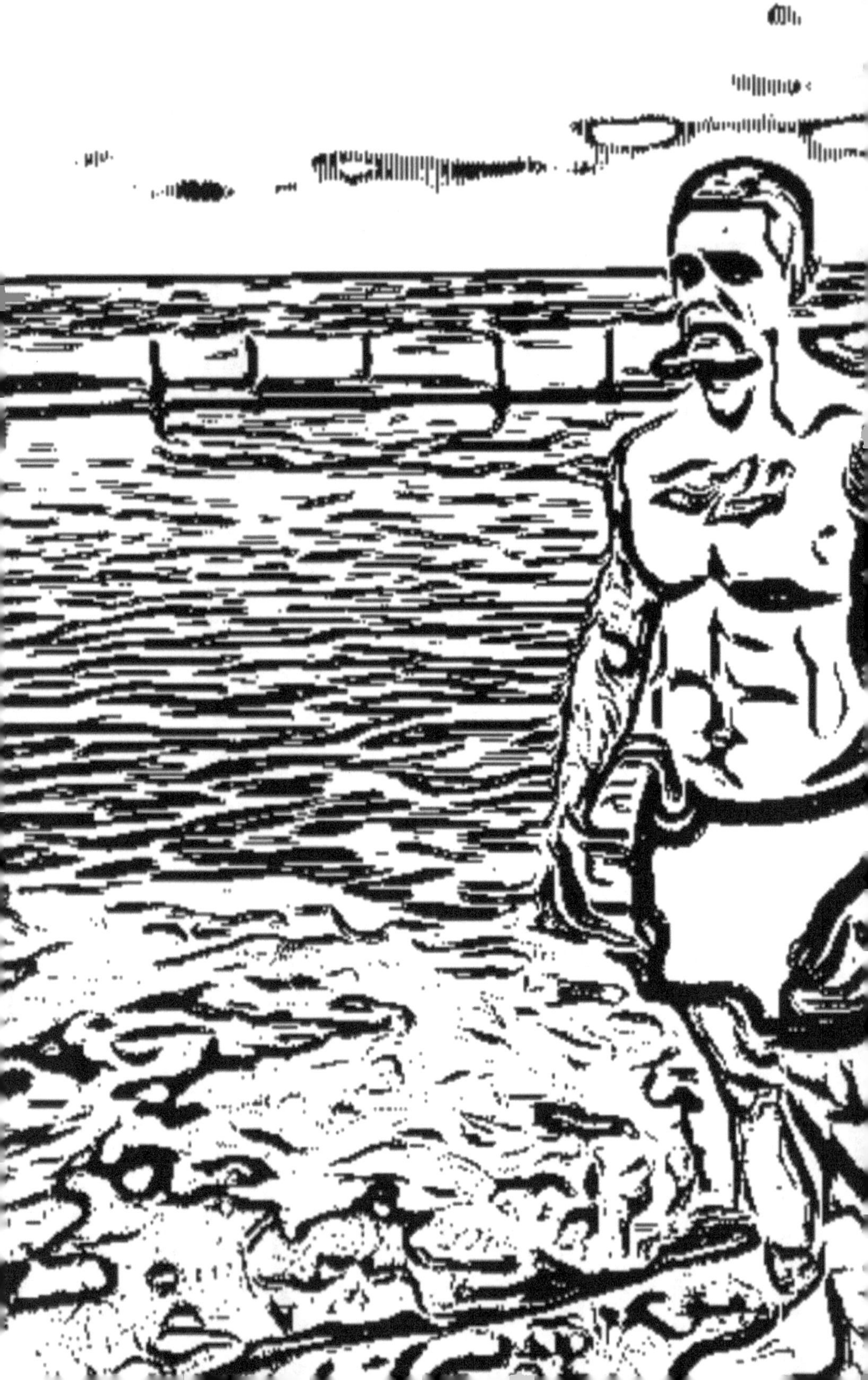

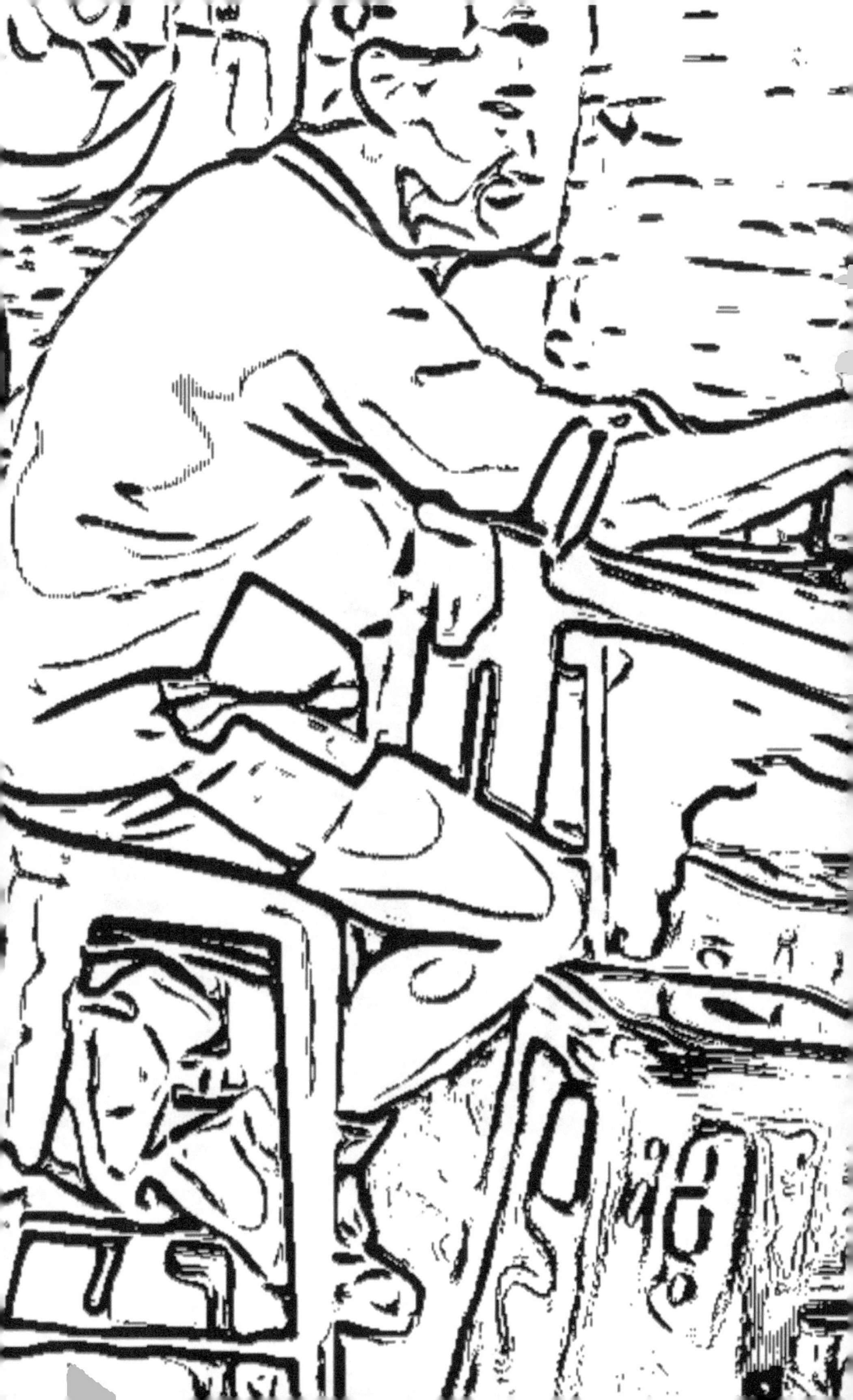

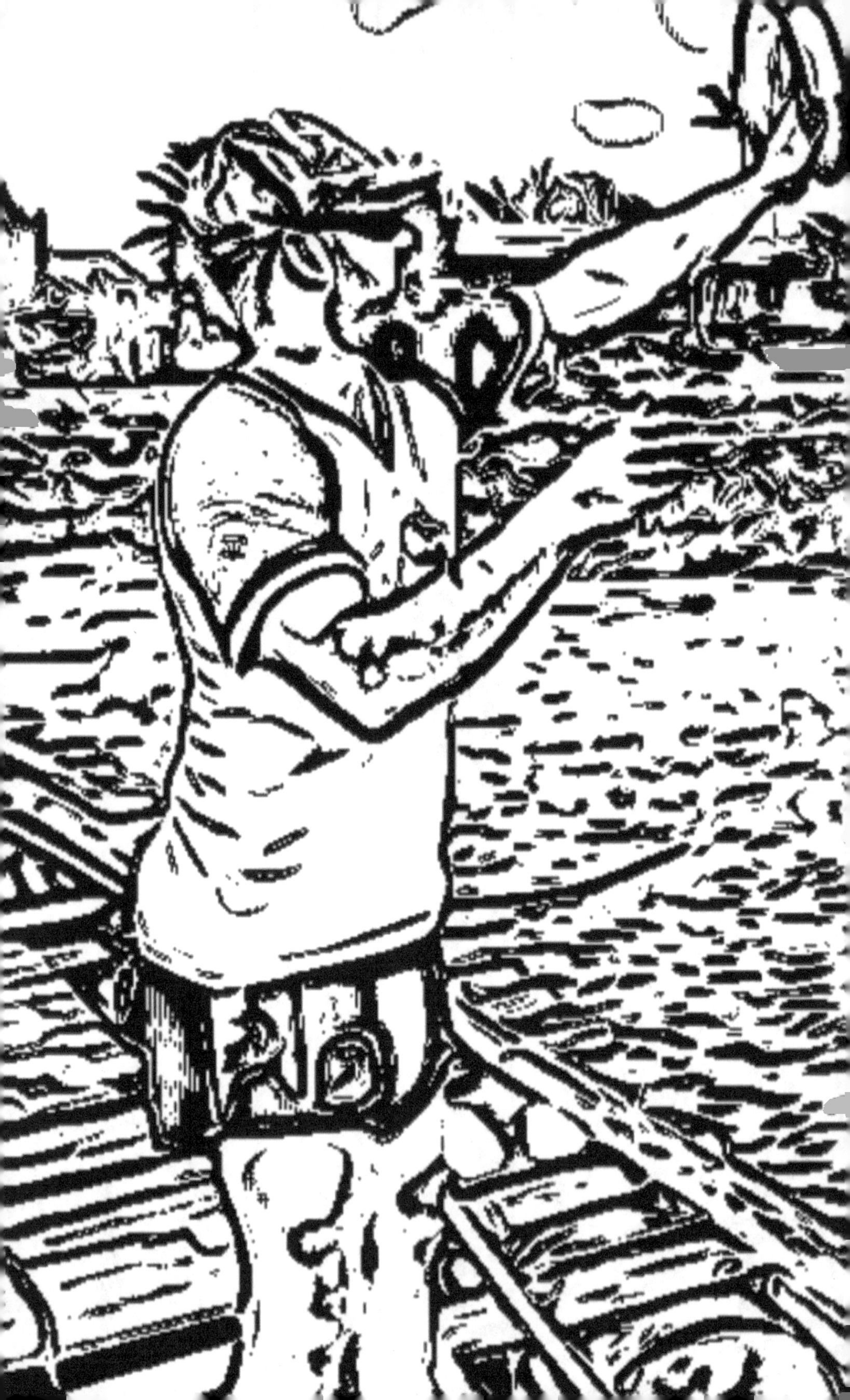

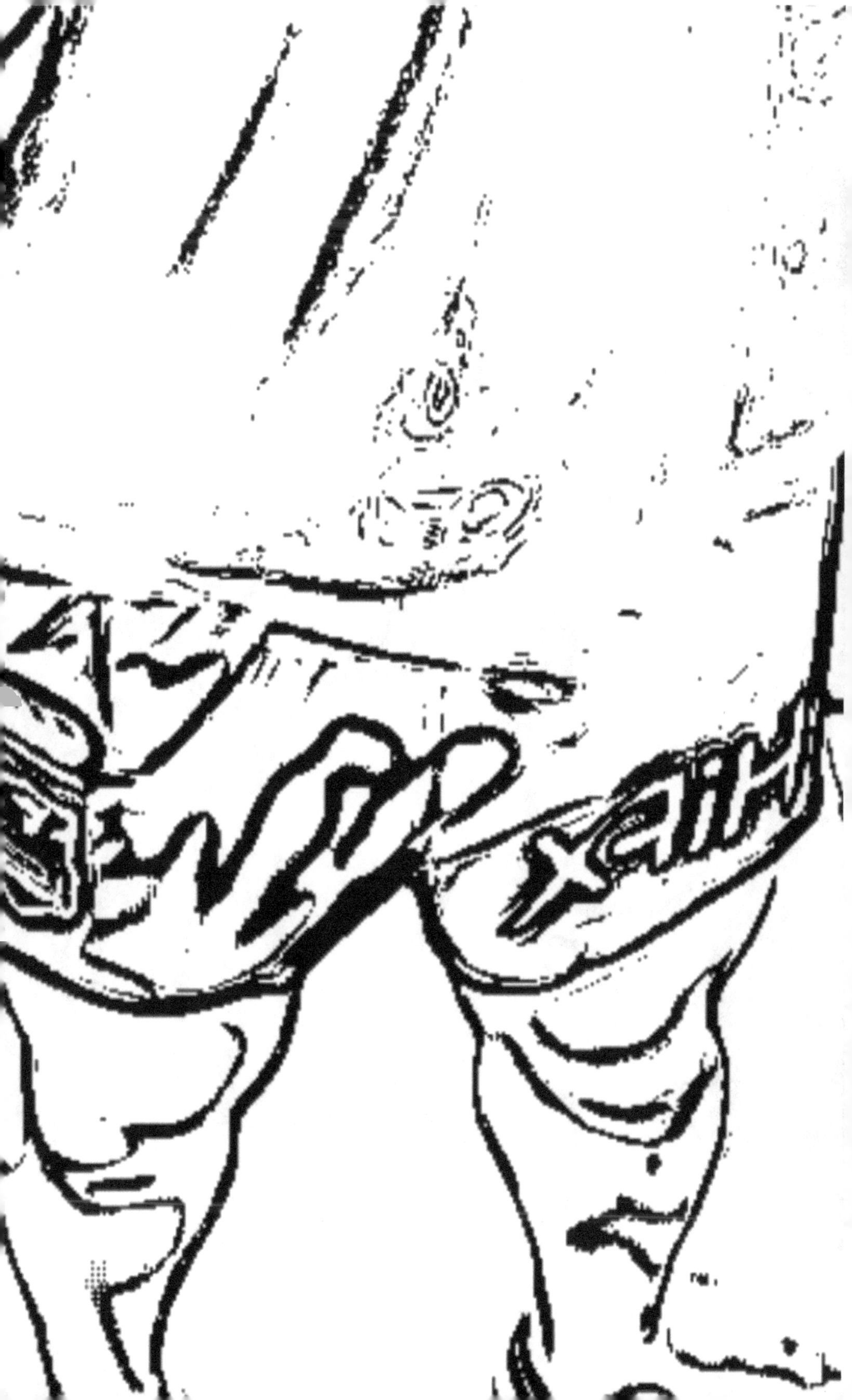

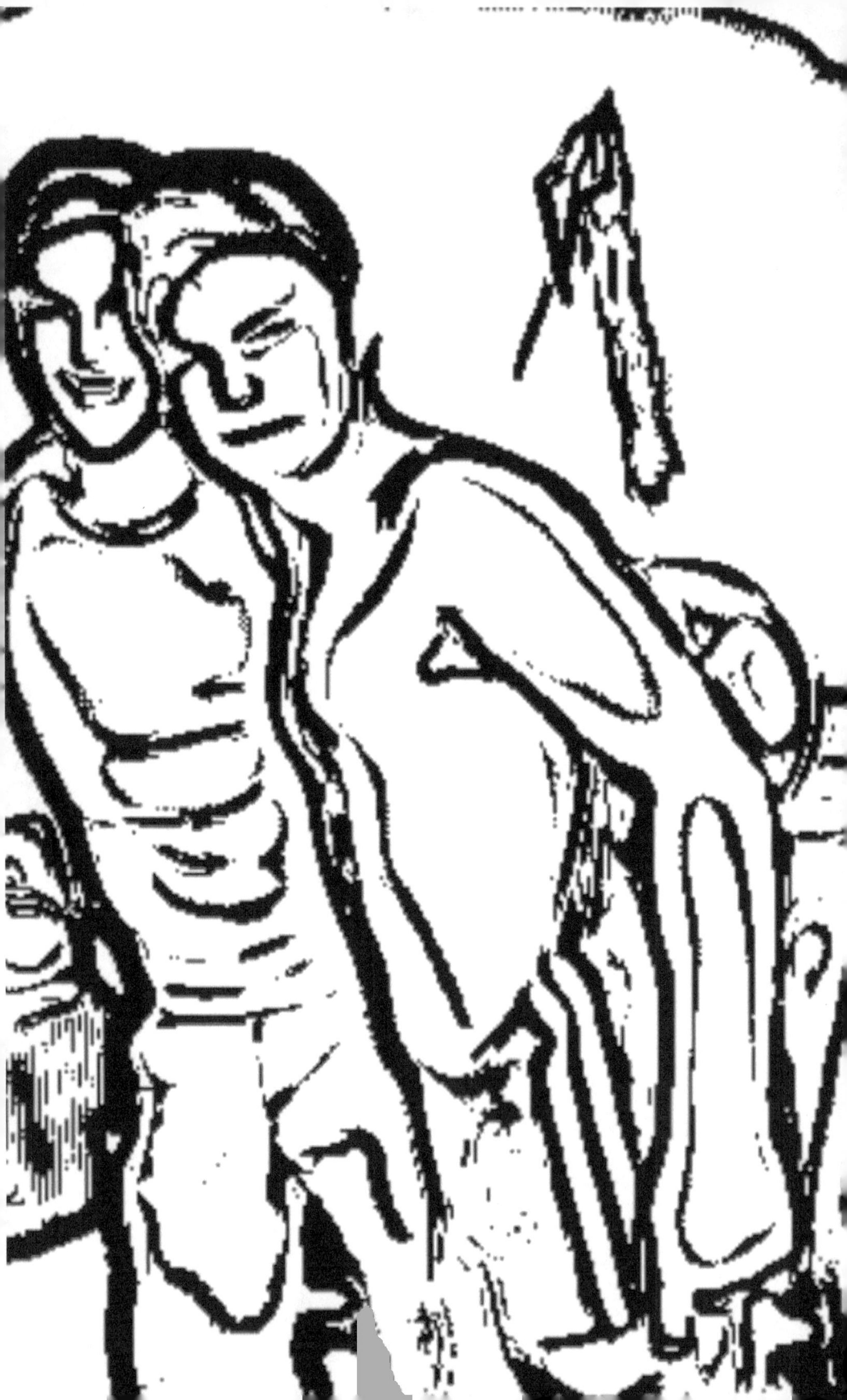

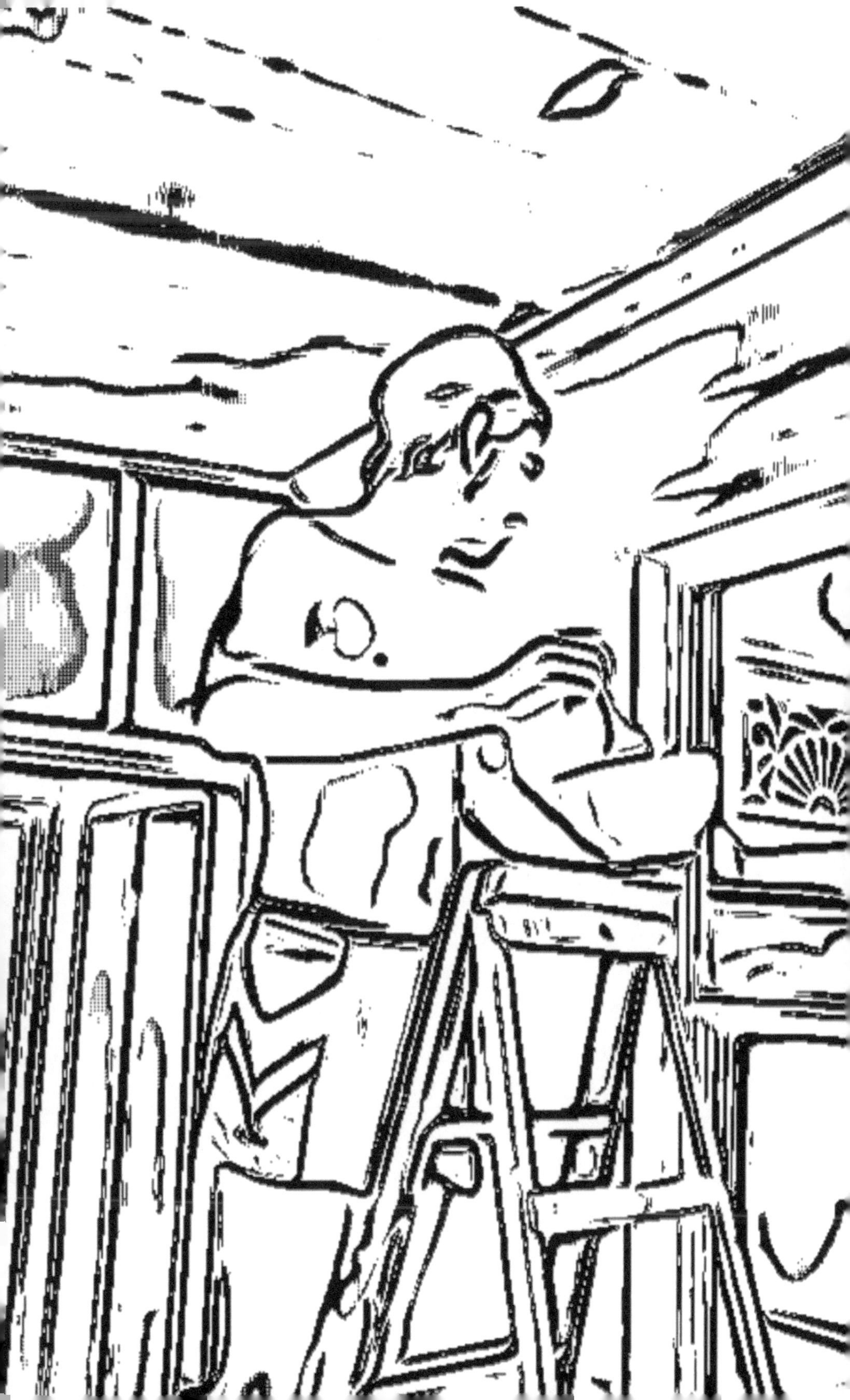

www.ingramcontent.com/pod-product-compliance
Lightning Source LLC
Chambersburg PA
CBHW021046180526
45163CB00005B/2304
* 9 7 8 0 3 5 9 9 8 2 6 5 3 *